The Way of Gaia

Published by NatureCulture LLC

www.nature-culture.net

Copyright © 2023
by Martin Bridge and Steve Trombulak

ISBN: 978-1-7375740-8-8

Library of Congress Control Number: 2022951458

Cover Art and Design:
Martin Bridge
www.thebridgebrothers.com

Interior Design:
Steve Trombulak, Martin Bridge, and Lis McLoughlin

The Way of Gaia

Art by Martin Bridge
Words by Steve Trombulak

Published by
NatureCulture LLC
Northfield, MA

Contents

Entering *The Way of Gaia*
A Foreword by John Davis

The late wildlands philanthropist Doug Tompkins said,
"If anything can save the world, I'd put my money on
beauty."* To this I would add that beauty comes best at
the confluence of art and science, which together help us
understand and protect the wild world around us.

The Way of Gaia is an astonishingly beautiful book, with
writings by conservation biologist Steve Trombulak
and paintings by artist Martin Bridge. At a time when
many need relief from the ongoing grief of accelerating
environmental and humanitarian crises, *The Way of Gaia*
lifts spirits and inspires action for our beleaguered home.
While spiritually guided, it is scientifically grounded and
bears witness not just to the great beauty but also the great
tragedy we see around us every day.

This meditation on the wonder of life on Earth reminds us
that we are kin to all creatures, that we are all comprised of
Earth, Air, Fire, and Water; and that Movement is central
to our being. Bridge and Trombulak share the insights
of biologists who have disclosed the urgent need of wild
creatures to be free to move widely to meet their needs.

Those of us devoted to rewilding—to helping protect big
wild places and restore missing species—will especially
appreciate the portrayal of predation: a critical part of life,
but one from which people have detached themselves,
getting food from supermarkets rather than directly from
the land. We all take lives, but killing ceases to be part of
the Way when causing unnecessary harm.

---

* Butler, T. and Lubarsky, S. 2017. *On Beauty: Douglas R. Tompkins—
Aesthetics and Activism*. Berkeley, CA: David Brower Center. 110.

Likewise inspiring is the entry on Kingdoms, sketching the basics of life as we understand them. Getting to know our wild neighbors is the first step in rejoining the community of life on Earth; and *The Way of Gaia* poignantly paints the Tree of Life, from which we are recklessly lopping branches.

When loved ones are lost, eulogies are needed; Forever Gone is a piece to read repeatedly to help end this biological crisis. This bittersweet poem bears witness to some of the most endangered of the countless species that our actions are driving to extinction.

Realistic yet hopeful, the authors succeed in celebrating life and expressing gratitude rather than hectoring for failing to avert these crises. Too many books on the grim conditions of today leave readers with little hope. In contrast, *The Way of Gaia* invites us to slow down, meet our wild neighbors, and take to the streets to speak for them.

Particularly challenging for some may be the concept of the Anthropocene. At an extreme, the notion suggests Earth has been so modified by humans, nothing is "natural" anymore and the Wild need not be protected. *The Way of Gaia* underscores a more humble view that humans need to help nature heal and rejoin the biotic community.

Our species has become alienated from Gaia, causing unnecessary harm to millions of other life forms every day. *The Way of Gaia* teaches us to live again gently—in Aldo Leopold's words—as "plain members" of the biotic community. We need a new story that places us within, not above, the biosphere and teaches us to reign in our destructive tendencies. *The Way of Gaia* is a beginning for a healing, restorative, rewilding story.

—John Davis, January 2023

The Way of Gaia is the Way Home
A Foreword by Andras Corban-Arthen

A very long time ago, the Greek lyric poet Simonides of Ceos reportedly said that "a poem is a painting that speaks, and a painting is a poem that has no words." Those two art forms blend and complement each other splendidly in *The Way of Gaia*, the inspired collaboration between a painter—Martin Bridge—and a poet—Steve Trombulak—who bring their singular gifts to bear upon the complex relationship between humanity and the natural world.

The authors have been my dear friends for many years. We all met through our involvement with the EarthSpirit Community, an organization which I founded in the 1970s with the aim of developing Earth-centered culture, spirituality, and community. Steve and Martin, despite coming from rather different backgrounds, nevertheless shared an affinity with these aims, and our community provided a fertile common ground to help nurture the realization of this book.

Both Martin and Steve identify themselves as animists, as do I. Animism is an ancient spiritual modality in which all of the natural world is perceived as alive, sentient, and ensouled. It does not rely on dogma, on anthropomorphic deities, on revelation or blind faith. Instead, animism seeks a direct and unfettered experience of reality that transcends the boundaries of language and reason, of explanations and definitions, to engage a more expansive and enhanced awareness. It is rooted in an understanding that humans are not at all separate from Nature, and that we exist as part of an interdependent web which binds all beings of the Earth; in short, that the Earth does not belong to us, but rather, that we belong to the Earth. It also proposes that, at the heart of the universe, there is a Great Mystery which neither religion nor science has come close to unraveling because, by its very nature, it defies explanation: it can only truly be *experienced*.

At a time when the anthropocentric, monotheistic and materialistic standards of Western civilization have brought us face-to-face with the dismal prospect of multiple global catastrophes, animism can provide us with a very different perspective, a very different story, a very different course of action. The greed, the arrogance, and the apathy which fuel these current crises arise from deep-seated notions of how the world works or should work, of how we have been conditioned to respond to the most profound existential questions that have such a strong bearing upon our individual and collective behavior. Nothing changes unless we change. The authors of *The Way of Gaia* are deeply mindful of our need for changing paradigms, and in this book they apply their considerable skills to blend images, words, spirituality, and science to offer us much-needed guidance and clear sight.

Though Martin Bridge is primarily a painter, it would be far more accurate to describe him as a visionary artist. His images depict the world not as we ordinarily see it but, rather, as we don't see it: he opens doorways to show us the shape of the world as he experiences it beyond the boundaries of ordinary human perception. His works are imbued with a remarkably primal, entheogenic quality that draws on patterns of the natural world such as spirals, spheres, webs, and branches, and renders them very much alive and in constant motion: they swirl, and flow, and throb with atavistic echoes of *Lascaux*, of *Altamira*. They reveal the underlying spiritual force that permeates all things, that brings the universe, and its myriad configurations of reality, into being.

Steve Trombulak has had a long and celebrated career as a scientist, having served as a Professor of Environmental Studies for several decades. At heart, though, Steve is truly a poet, with the ability to weave interlacing webs of words, tendrils of meaning that reach for each other and bring us along and bind us to our best selves. In *The Way of Gaia*, his prose-poems inspire, challenge, counsel, remind us of what we should never forget, lift the covers off our fears and invite us to dance with them, offer us clarity and wise teachings, and reassure us that we are not—can never truly be—alone because we are inescapably bound to each other, bound to all beings of the Earth, and that, in the end, we are most certainly everywhere, we are indeed everything.

The Way of Gaia is the remarkable gift of two remarkable men. Their paintings that speak, their poems without words, shine a welcome light upon a path which, in these trying times, can lead us toward hope, toward the soul-strength necessary to effect our healing, to find a greater peace and a place of real belonging. To follow the Way of Gaia is to follow the Way Home.

—Andras Corban-Arthen
January 2023

Biographies of Foreword Contributors

John Davis is the executive director of The Rewilding Institute and a rewilding advocate on the staff of the Adirondack Council, where he previously served as conservation director. He is the author of *Big, Wild, and Connected: Scouting an Eastern Wildway from Florida to Quebec* (Island Press, 2015); *Split Rock Wildway: Scouting the Adirondack Park's Most Diverse Wildlife Corridor* (Essex Editions, 2017); *Rewilding Earth Unplugged* and *Rewilding Earth Best of 2019* (Essex Editions, 2018 and 2019), editor of the website *Rewilding Earth* and co-editor of the book *Rewilding North America* (Island Press, 2004) by Dave Foreman. His eight months spent hiking the proposed 5,000-mile Wildway from Mexico to Canada are the subject of the 2017 film, *Born to Rewild*. Davis is a co-founder of The Wildlands Project (now Wildlands Network) and Wild Farm Alliance.

Andras Corban-Arthen, founder and spiritual director of the EarthSpirit Community, is also president of the European Congress of Ethnic Religions headquartered in Vilnius, Lithuania. He sits on the advisory council of the Ecospirituality Foundation, a United Nations Consultative NGO in Italy, and served for thirteen years on the board of the Parliament of the World's Religions. Originally from Galiza, Spain, he has taught about the indigenous European pagan traditions throughout the U.S. and abroad since the 1970s. He was chosen to represent those traditions at the United Nations Interfaith Conference on Religion and Prejudice in 1991; and he has been a featured presenter at the Parliaments of the World's Religions, the Encuentro Mundial Interreligioso, the Diálogo Cultural Universal, the Religions for the Earth conference, and the concurrent People's Climate March, in NYC.

An Invitation
from the Authors

Regardless of one's spiritual beliefs, it is impossible to deny that humans are unique on the Earth. Not because of our sentient awareness—many animals, from our fellow primates to octopuses show similar abilities. Not because of our ability to learn from experience and pass that knowledge on across generations, since chimpanzees also practice generational learning. Not because of our capacity for self-recognition; we share this ability with orcas and even ants. And certainly not because of our ability to use tools. Many social animals, including elephants, dolphins, and crows, will shape found objects and do something useful with them.

Our uniquity comes from the types of tools we make and the scale of their precision and impact in both space and time. Dams made of concrete, chain saws, gas-powered engines, musical instruments, bulldozers, agricultural plows, skyscrapers, inorganic fertilizer, jet engines, photovoltaic cells, Earth-orbiting satellites, stethoscopes … the list is long of shaped objects unique to our species that we use toward some end.

Our uniquity comes as well from the ends we choose. Throughout human history, we have used tools to conform the Earth toward our own goals, such as producing food, obtaining water, creating shelter, and storing energy. These goals in and of themselves can understandably be admired. Human flourishing, in fact humanity's very survival, depended throughout history on achieving them consistently and reliably.

When humanity was only thinly settled across the planet, our transformation of Earth's life-giving natural systems was well within the biosphere's ability to regenerate. But as our numbers grew and our tools became more sophisticated, we crossed the threshold of Earth's resilience.

In the present day, some measures show that over half of the habitable land on Earth has already been directly converted to some form of agriculture, with much of the remaining transformed and fragmented by roads, cities, mining, and logging. In just 60 years, the concentration of carbon dioxide in the atmosphere has increased by nearly 25%, leading to measurable increases in global temperatures, storm intensity, sea level, and acidification of the oceans' waters. The rate of species extinction is arguably between 1,000 and 10,000 times higher than it would be under natural conditions. And some groups of organisms and communities—such as pollinators, carnivores, coral reefs, and old growth forests—have borne the brunt of this biodepletion, being particularly vulnerable to the effects of pollution or targeted for extirpation. Further, conservatively 10% of the world's human population faces food insecurity, while 25% faces the same crisis with water.

All these stresses, and dozens more just like them, challenge the natural systems of Earth to replenish themselves through regenerative cycles and to allow the continued existence of the several million other species who also call this planet home. Detailed measurements of what humanity extracts from or emits into the lands and waters each year compared to Earth's capacity to renew itself show that humanity has been living beyond planetary limits since at least the 1980s. If we were talking about comparing withdrawals to interest earned in a bank account, we'd say that we've been drawing down the principle of the account for a long time and are on an inexorable path to draining it completely.

Why did we allow this to happen when clearly it threatens the survival of humanity as well as much of the more-than-just-human world? Fundamentally, it was because humanity lost sight of its true relationship to the Earth. We confused what we *could* do with our tools with what we *should* do. And in the process, we crafted a narrative of dominance that places humanity at the center of all life, where the rest of the planet exists solely as a collection of "resources" to serve us—without respect for the physical and biological laws of nature, without respect for more-than-just-human life, without limit, without end.

In some traditions, Earth is seen as being only a temporary home—a stopover on a journey to a place for eternal life. In others, short-term acquisition and gratification through exploitation take precedence over long-term stewardship and self-restraint. And in others, Earth systems, such as the atmosphere and oceans, are considered "externalities," able to absorb harmful consequences and byproducts of material production without limits or caution. The narrative of dominance—regardless of its philosophical justification—has been the overwhelming guide for humanity, especially in the last few centuries, on how the Earth and even ourselves could be treated.

But this is only a narrative, not destiny. We can choose a different narrative, one that realigns our senses of self, species identity, and place on Earth as being part of a vast network of life linked together across generational time by relationships of shared ancestry, beauty, and interdependence.

It is a narrative that calls for us to live as a part of Earth's biosphere. To live within the body of Gaia.

Gaia. Mother Earth. The planet. By any name, she (as indeed many cultures around the world and throughout time identify Earth as female due to her capacity to bear life) is our home. She feeds us and gives us water to drink and the materials to make shelter from the elements. She has brought forth the rich diversity of life that forms a web of connections, a web in which we have always been a part. She has been our teacher, our protector, and our guide. And just as we feel toward our birth mothers, we have a responsibility to treat her with respect.

The purpose of this book is to call to mind, through both art and prose, a form and texture for this narrative. Here you will find offerings crafted in shape, color, and words that invite us all to see and understand with mind, heart, and soul our true connections with the Web of Life. They offer new ways of thinking for those who are grounded in the narratives of destruction, as well as for those who already know that a narrative of constructive holism is needed but seek words and images of affirmation.

We the authors hope these lessons and prayers—read singly as a focus for contemplation or altogether as a manifesto for a new way of living—will affirm, inspire, and contribute to replacing the destructive narratives with frames that will lead us all to honor and restore life on this sacred Earth, and to the flourishing of all life without end.

—Steve Trombulak & Martin Bridge
December 2022

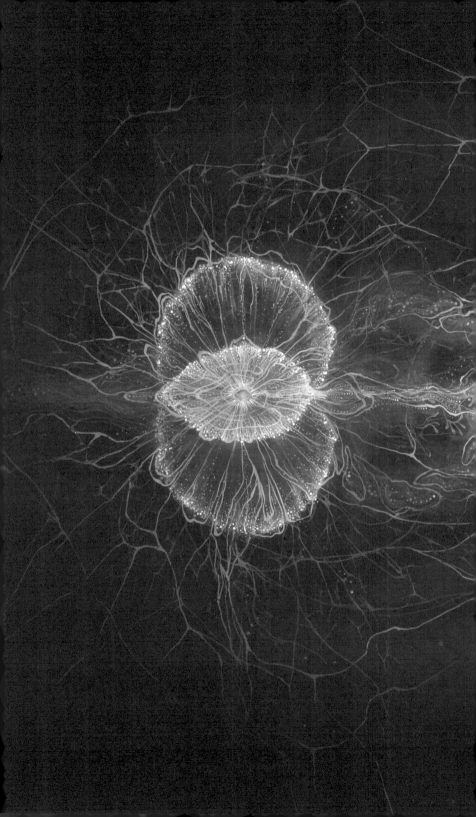

The Tree of Life

Settle in – take a seat or kneel or stand
and prepare yourself to see the Way.

You may think the most important search
for you is to find an answer

to the question, "Who am I?"
But I tell you now that this is wrong.

Important yes, but not the most,
because you cannot learn who you are

unless you know from where you came.
First you must ask, "Who is my family,

the ones who travel with me on this Path,
the ones with whom I claim a kin line?"

Settle in – and come to understand.

Be still now and reach out past the obvious:
the kin of your youth, your home, your seed.

Reach out further and feel your line expand
to hold your neighbors, your tribe, your culture.

Go yet further still and connect to those who
share your country, language, history, beliefs.

And now reach past them to those who are different,
for make no mistake, we are all different – all unique.

See that which binds us all as family, the codes
that weave us together as the people of humanity,

sharing all our ways for being in the world:
how we sense, move, eat, give birth, and grow.

This line is wide, but family is yet larger still.
Reach out further to those who are *almost* like you,

different yet family still by the codes shared
for the gears of digestion, hair, and reproduction.

Further now and feel the kinship born of shared code
for respiration and bones
    for nerves and growth
        for the alliance of cells
            for their internal structure
                for the very genes themselves in their
                    form, division, and means of replication.

And here we come now to the truth on which the Path rests.

We are kin to all of life, each of us tracing our
line back through ancestors to the ancestors before

and before even that, each one descended
from the Great Ancestor of all, the one

who lit the first spark of life, took root, and spread
branches up through time and across Gaia's skin,

spiraling up into millions of millions of branches,
together becoming the Tree of Life.

2

There are those who look up at the stars and ask –
"Are humans alone in this Universe?"

But look around you here on Gaia, our Mother
the Earth, and understand this: *We have never been.*

This is who you are, a branch on a magnificent Tree,
the family of all life with whom you walk the Path.

And the branches intertwine in myriads of ways,
creating stories of mutual transformation.

The journeys of all are bound together in both life
and death, as is happiness, peace, and balance for

us now and for all the kin who follow after.
Come, this is the Way of Gaia.

Morning Prayer

As I walk this path, I pray for all those who walk with me.

First, I pray for myself.

May I meet my responsibility to be an honest caretaker of my body and soul. May I find the wisdom to remember that each thought and action is a choice, and by my choices I shape both the path and how I walk it.

I pray for my family.

May I meet my responsibility to support them on their journeys along their own paths. May I find the serenity to help them when it is needed and to show loving kindness in every moment.

I pray for the community of all humanity.

May I meet my responsibility to join with them to make our community safe and healthy in all ways. May I find the serenity to refrain from ill thoughts, choosing instead to practice loving kindness. May I find the grace to think of others before I think of myself, giving who I am to the community more than asking the community to give itself to me.

Finally, I pray for the community of All Beings.

May I meet my responsibility to speak for those who cannot speak for themselves and recall that rightness is found within the integrity of the world. May I find ways to strengthen my focus so I may see more of the world with open eyes, hear more of the world with open ears, and hold more of the world in my heart and mind.

As I walk this path, I pray for all those who walk with me.

By the earth that is my body, the water that is my blood, the air that is my breath, and the fire that is my spirit …

I commit myself this day and every day to
      honor life,
      protect life, and
      restore life
      wheresoever it may be
      on this sacred Earth.

So may it be.

Keeping Time

The Earth sings a rhythmic line,
never resting, raising vibrations
that hold from ocean to sky.

Slow pulses measured in hours and days,
solstice to solstice to solstice again
across epochs and ages since the first dawn.

No one knows for sure how Gaia sings
her song, if by winds pushing water,
the churning of magma,

the movement of her skin faulting
along lines ancient and deep,
or a welling of her soul out into the void.

Keeping time ▬
      Keeping time ▬
         Keeping time ▬

All life is born into this hum, a background
song of our birth, breath, and death.
We're not simply surrounded by

her vibrations, we are infused with them.
They lie beneath our heartbeat,
our inspiration, the division of our cells,

the dancing of atoms across membranes
and skin. Even time's flow is marked
by the frequency of transitions in atomic states.

We don't just feel her rhythm, as if bearing
witness to its push on our senses from an
elsewhere. It is always a part of who we are,

when we sleep and dream, sit quiet streamside
to watch the first light of day, or stand
motionless as birds fly overhead.

Let go of expectations of remaining at rest
and let your life be a dance set to the tempo
of the vibrations within.

Keeping time ▬
　　　Keeping time ▬
　　　　　Keeping time ▬

Time's Arrow

The Universe moves toward disorder

Proving time's arrow with
    t-i-c-k and t-o-c-k but not also k-c-i-t and k-c-o-t

Gaia's body ever changing and us along with her
with more ways   to   glide into   chaos

A natural state
                    of things as pieces
pull apart
atoms cells   soil
                  relationships   homes
mountains stars   galaxies

∞

Yet pay the tax   on energy flow and
another state
                     emerges on
    order's one-way street
pushing against stasis   complacency
    instability
Promoting
    pattern   structure   innovation
    gears that function in the engines of life
    new forms living new lives in new ways

      Opposing chaos with energy
        becomes purpose
          in life

These Four Things

Metal, sun, sea, breath, and skin
Winter snow, mist, sulphur, salt
Typhoon, glacier, silt, and spit
Quantum state, spring breeze, and rain

Mucus, muscle, burning wood
Exhalate, magnetic core
Ozone, semen, mud, and tear
Humus, lymph, vibration, blood

Everything of value that makes
Gaia's body or moves us toward
More sacred union with all beings
Calls attention to what's at stake
If our actions don't match our words
Yet are made from just these four things

Earth

In every moment, let me give thanks to Earth.

Gratitude for the silence and stillness of stone.
Gratitude for the minerals of my body.
Gratitude for the soil that grows my food.
Gratitude for the ore that allows me to build.
Gratitude for the colors, shapes, and textures that surround me.
Gratitude for the vastness of the land and the intimacy of its details.
Gratitude for the solid ground on which l stand, holding me up with each step and dance.
Gratitude for the formation of life in both its symmetry and chaos.
Gratitude for the foundations of fields and forests.
Gratitude for the basins of oceans and seas.
Gratitude for the ever-present reminder of impermanence in uncertain times yet grounding in this moment and place.
Gratitude for the lesson of destruction that makes room for renewal and what is to come.
Gratitude for holding our bodies in death.

With gratitude I see that what I have is enough.

Gratitude to Earth.

Air

In every moment, let me give thanks to Air.

Gratitude for my first breath, ushering me into life, for the final breath that will mark my passage, and for the gift of all the breaths that come between.
Gratitude for the coo of a child, the whisper of a lover, and the wisdom of a poet.
Gratitude for the moments that take my breath away in awe and joy.
Gratitude for the inspiration to welcome change.
Gratitude for the exhalation that comes when I let go of what stands in my way.
Gratitude for the fuel that feeds my hearth fires.
Gratitude for the wind that carries the songs and prayers of my community.
Gratitude for spreading seeds for the Green Ones.
Gratitude for the medium within which the Winged Ones fly.
Gratitude for the calling of wild animals and the rustling of leaves in the trees.
Gratitude for winds that cool and winds that warm and winds that seed the clouds for rain.
Gratitude for its blanket of warmth and protection from light, which makes life with Gaia possible.

With gratitude I see that what I have is enough.

Gratitude to Air.

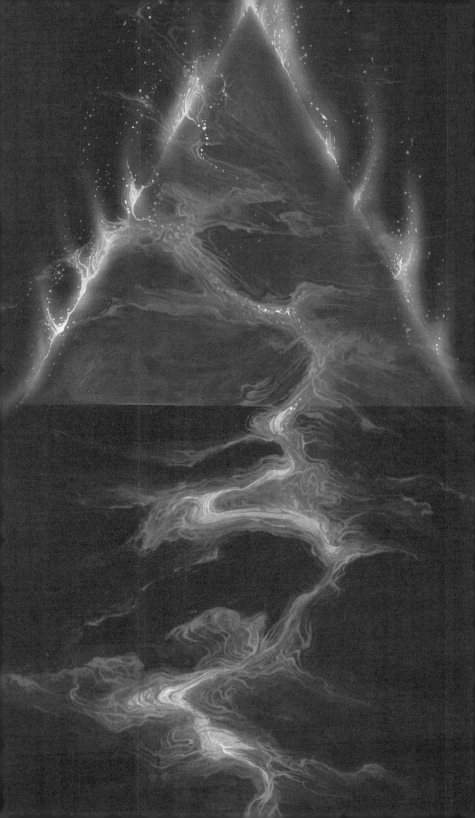

Fire

In every moment, let me give thanks to Fire.

Gratitude for the fire of the Sun, whose heat and light feeds
all life on Earth.

Gratitude for the metabolic furnace of my cells that warms
my blood and gives me the power for action.

Gratitude for the transformation of my food, baking bread
and loosening sinew to allow its nutrition to enter my
body.

Gratitude for the warmth of fire that burns through the
rhythmic night.

Gratitude for the light that shows me the faces of my
friends and family.

Gratitude for the sparks that shoot free like stars into the
sky.

Gratitude for the cascading chain of energy that powers
the tools that create homes, grow food, transport water,
and save lives.

Gratitude for the clearing of land and the restoration of life
to the forests and plains.

Gratitude for the burning spirit that drives me toward
justice.

With gratitude I see that what I have is enough.

Gratitude to Fire.

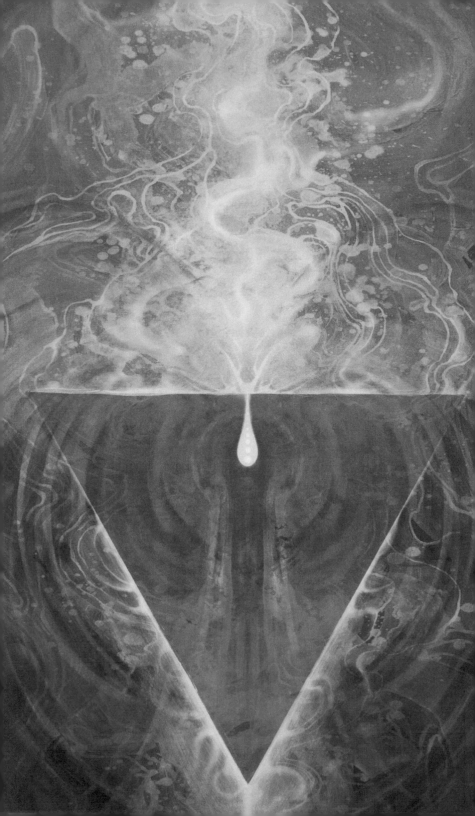

Water

In every moment, let me give thanks to Water.

Gratitude for the salted cocoon that held me within my
mother's body.
Gratitude for blood and lymph, sustaining my own body's
life.
Gratitude for the birthplace of the Tree of Life.
Gratitude for fluids strong enough to carve canyons and
smooth the rough edges of stone and skin.
Gratitude for the clouds that insulate the land and bring
rains to feed my crops.
Gratitude for snow and ice, refreshing the land across
seasons and millenniums.
Gratitude for rivers and streams, speaking with the voice
of currents and eddies.
Gratitude for the realm of the oceans, cradle of life and
light, depths and darkness, whale songs, coral reefs,
and the lungs of the world.
Gratitude for tender tears that can break down walls built
from wounds and fear.
Gratitude for the warm embrace of the water as I slide into
its wholeness, caressing my skin, buoying my body,
lifting my spirit, and healing my heart.

With gratitude I see that what I have is enough.

Gratitude to Water.

Movement

Nothing remains at rest.

Water flows as deep ocean rivers, measured in speeds
of only inches per day and in roiling ridges crashing
down where the land intrudes into its endless flow.

Flame weaves dancing arms upward from trunk and
leaf, sweeping blankets across wooded hillsides and
down like water from the mouths of volcanoes.

Air courses across membranes in each living being,
across the water's surface and the arms of the fire,
circling Gaia again and again since her beginnings.

And the Earth ... and the Earth.
Even with her, nothing remains at rest.

The spinning core, a buried dynamo creating
magnetic bands that stretch far out into the void
capturing the Sun's ejecta and firing the night sky.

The creeping mantle, its plastic flow rising and
falling, encasing the core and penetrating the land as
hot spots moving water, fire, and air.

The rafting crust, spreading wide and sinking deep,
pushing through with many names on many paths,
sharp elbows quaking a thousand times each day.

Rearranging the face of the Earth inches at a time,
spreading shockwaves and ever flowing across
millenniums of millenniums.

And then there is you.

Stand and imagine like a dream that you are at rest.
Will everything you can with all that you have
into stillness.

Pretend to yourself that you have become a
singularity of pure consciousness – motionless,
serene, and empty of all momentum.

And then …

Notice the air of your breath and the fire of your cells,
hear the blood in your veins, legacy of ocean waters
from where you came and where you will return.

Become aware of the crustal plate upon which you
stand and imagine its forceful journey
as Gaia's shifting skin.

You riding as a passenger graced to witness
earthquake after earthquake, a language and
grammar of Gaia's long story.

And come to know that even you are not at rest
and can never be. Be at peace, for movement
and change are the natural order of things.

Spread and course yourself with gentleness.
Flow and dance with grace. The Way calls you
to ride the earthquakes of crust and life,

large and small, with awe and gratitude,
and bear witness each day to the living Earth.

Cycles Within Cycles

Do not worry if the line of your life
does not appear to be straight.
No line ever is, and your path has no choice
but to wind among the cycles of nature.

Day flows into night back into day,
and the tilted Earth spinning on its axis
carries you along with it, entraining
your body's rhythm with its own demands.

Overtaken by sleep and driven awake,
your body heat rising and falling, heart racing
forward and falling back, all driven by
the master clock in your Earth-born brain.

Over this cycle of the Earth's untiring spin lies
the longer cycle of the Moon's endless journey,
its single night and day measured coarsely across
your month, newly full to fully new and back.

Cycles on Earth ever linked to the Moon's journey:
the flow of a woman's blood and the ocean's waters,
internal thoughts of rage and despair, and the low
silent grinding of mountain rock on rock.

And as the Moon does its pirouette,
the tilted Earth does its own around the Sun,
pulling you and all of life through seasons,
a dark time flowing slowly into the light.

Days lengthen, mood brightens,
land and waters greening and growing
as light gives fuel for renewal and rebirth,
feeding all even as days move again into dark.

Day upon day, month upon month,
year upon year upon year, light into dark
into light again, you ride this cosmological path,
never straight, but always true.

And Earth cycles drive those of life and land
beyond your own short span of years, as wobbles
in the shape of its orbit and angles of tilt across
hundreds of millenniums shape all else on the ride.

Summers of cold strung together year after year,
into winters of heat unchanged from the summer,
driving the flow and decay of ice across the land
and across the seas, and what it means to be on Earth.

The ground scraped bare by miles-thick ice sheets
exposed again across the cycle, allowing fresh birth of
soil. Ice packs retreating poleward and winterward,
freeing the surface again to light, air, water, and fire.

The line of your life is carried along, cycle within
cycle, given richness by the movement of the
endless rhythm of what it means to be alive
in this ever-sacred place.

These words for you

as you spin and flow:

Give thanks for the ride.

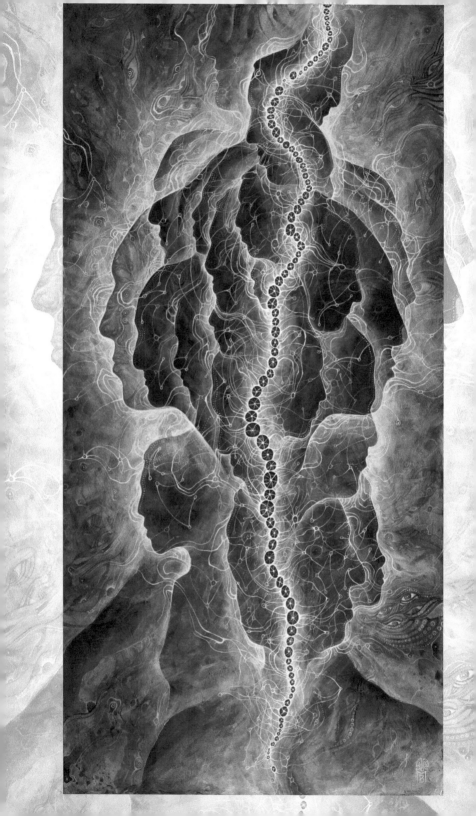

Great Ancestors

You

are a miracle of time and chance, the very end of a branch on the Tree of Life.

A bud at the tip of a twig at the end of a branchlet on a branch on a limb emerging from the trunk whose roots anchor fast at the dawn of life.

The span from the base of your bud to the roots of the Tree are the lives of your ancestors: your parents, their parents, back through the soulstream of generations before generations into the time when those parents could not even be called human but instead were the ancestors of all humanity: the Upright People.

And again further back through more generations of ancestors, the Southern Apes flowing down the soulstream to the Foundation Apes, joining with other ancestors: the First Primates, to the Mammal-forms, to the Ones with Dog-teeth, and into the Reptiles Like Mammals with Wedge-pointed Teeth.

Branches deeper down to the source, called by distant names faded from family memory: the Double-axed Reptiles, to Those of Solid Skulls, to our ancestors who first crawled out of the water, perhaps out of the Mother Ocean herself, like *Tiktaalik*, the Great Ancestor to all like us who walk the land with bones and muscle yet descendants themselves from all those who came before.

The Armored Ones of the Oceans, the children of the Ones Without Jaws, to the Ones Without Bones. Closer now to the roots of the Tree we come: the Ones Who Feed on Others, the First Ones with Many Cells, and deep further still back billions of years to the very First Cell, from whom the Tree was born.

These are your ancestors, generations beyond counting whose paths along the Way fit them to the world even as they shaped the world and each other.

The ones who survived as Gaia grew and changed through cycles of heat and cold, of wet and dry, of fiery skies of ash and death or placid winds. The ones who gave birth to next generations to add one more ring of growth on the Tree.

Leading up through all the limbs and branches to you and all the other buds out on the ends of today. The trillions upon trillions bound together in Gaia's Web, connected to all that lives.

Connected to all the ancestors.

Remember them well and in the remembering show gratitude for all those whose lives gave life to

You.

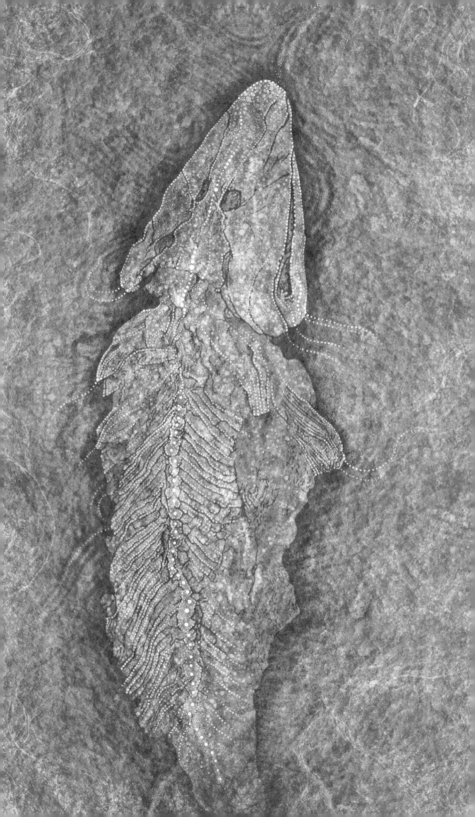

Kingdoms

Tracing a single line on the Tree of Life – from the tip of
a twig back through time, down along branchlets and
branches, past forks into trunks and deep into its ancient
roots – is hard.

Yet harder still is drawing with even the lightest degree
of certainty the shape of the entire Tree, each twig and
broken branch, each fork and root. Much of the pattern of
life's flourishing that emerged from the roots, the splitting
of one branch from another, is hidden to us, having
left behind only sporadic signals of its change weaving
through time.

And the signals are often confusing. We can see the
diversity of life in the present day – though sadly even that
view is incomplete – and we can catch occasional glimpses
of life's tapestry in the Before Times. But the further back
in time we cast our gaze, the more opaque the view.

We are left then simply to tell stories, the "if this, then that"
tales that help us form an image in our mind of what the
Tree in its fullness looks like and how it came to be shaped
over the billions of years since the first birth of life. These
are not stories conjured solely from baseless imaginings,
but stories grounded in what we see in the twigs of today
and the branches glimpsed through the fog that surrounds
the past.

If the *presence of a cell nucleus* is an important part of the
story of how the Tree grew, then those twigs who don't
have a nucleus are on a different trunk than those who do.

If *cells coming together to collaborate in creating a whole complex organism* is an important part of the story, then those cells who live on their own, apart from others, are …

If the *ability to use the energy of the Sun to create food* is an important part of the story, then …

If *this*, then *that*. And such forks in the telling give sight to our mind's eye and a shape to the Tree.

We tell stories based on what we know and – as important – on what we think it all means as to Gaia's growth and life's journey through time. And one of the stories we tell about the Tree goes something like this.

This is the story of the Five Kingdoms …

In the beginning was the Kingdom Monera, the First Ones:
Simple and solitary cells, they were —
and still are, in the many forms of bacteria
we share the Earth with —

able to live and reproduce but had no nucleus
to hold their single coiled strand of genetic information.

But after billions of years, some monerans developed
a membrane around their genetic coil and formed
the base of a new trunk on the Tree,
the Kingdom Protista, the Solitary Nucleated Ones:

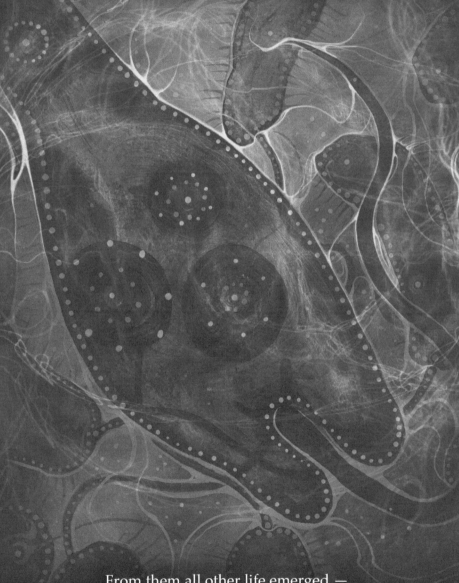

From them all other life emerged —
life made up of specialized, co-operating cells.

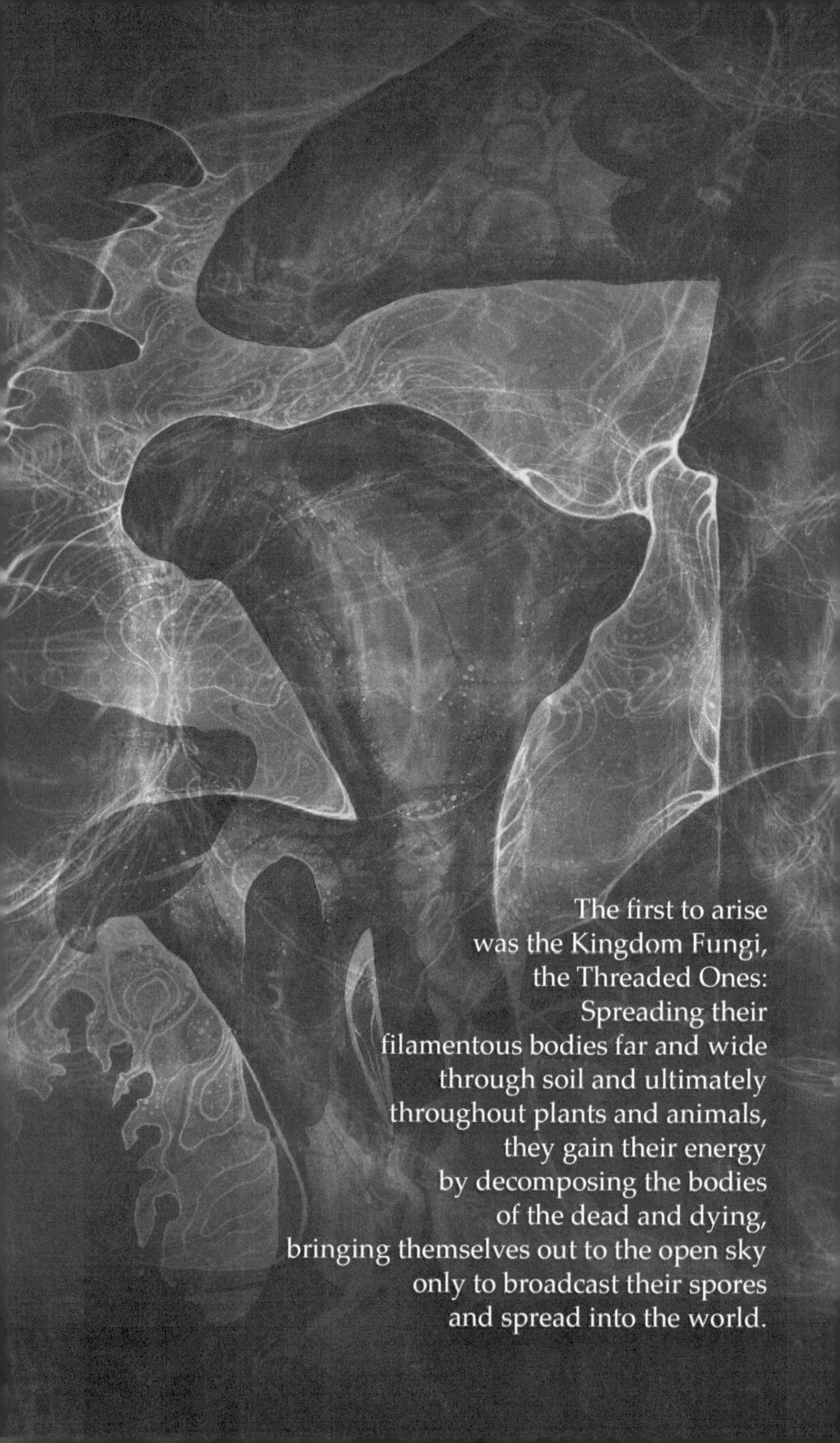

The first to arise
was the Kingdom Fungi,
the Threaded Ones:
Spreading their
filamentous bodies far and wide
through soil and ultimately
throughout plants and animals,
they gain their energy
by decomposing the bodies
of the dead and dying,
bringing themselves out to the open sky
only to broadcast their spores
and spread into the world.

Next came the Kingdom Plantae, the Green Ones:
First arising in the sea and eventually emerging
onto the land to root into the Earth,
they gain their energy for life
through the miracle of transforming
the light of the Sun into the complex
structures of their bodies, spores,
seeds, flowers, and fruit.

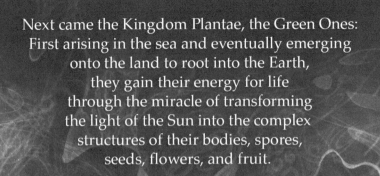

The diversity of the Green Ones is the story
of the diverse ways to seek the power of the Sun.

And finally came the Kingdom Animalia,
the Moving Ones: They travel freely everywhere

to gain their energy by consuming the bodies of others,
threaded, green, or those themselves who are on the move.
First arising in the waters as the Swimming Ones ...

… and later coming onto land as the Legged Ones,
Winged Ones, Climbing Ones, and Digging Ones.
And some of these, such as the whales and sea turtles,
returned to the sea to swim once again.

The myriad ways of movement emerged
from all the ways to find food and in turn
avoid becoming food for others.

Of course, this story of the Five Kingdoms is but one of many we could tell. Others would tell a similar story of Six Kingdoms, and others still of Eight Kingdoms, or Three, or Four, or Seven. But they all take the same form to describe the Tree:

In the beginning, the young Earth, Gaia in her infancy, was devoid of life. Then life emerged and over time evolved into a rich diversity of forms to take advantage in different ways of the gifts bestowed by both the Sun and Gaia herself.

The metaphors we use to picture the diversity of life on Earth are only that: metaphors. We can imagine diversity as a Tree, revealing kinships and transitions over time. And also as a Web, revealing connections and dependencies among All Beings of the Earth. So too are the stories we tell about the kingdoms simply yet importantly metaphors.

Are all the Monerans similar enough to each other to live in the same kingdom, or are there differences among them large enough to deserve their separation into kingdoms of their own? Answers will emerge and change over time as we become wiser and more aware of all with whom we share this planet. All these metaphors are incomplete, and all are true, giving us languages to fully embrace the diversity of all life.

But at the heart of our relationship with Gaia, what matters most is not how we describe the Tree, but how we treat it.

With respect.

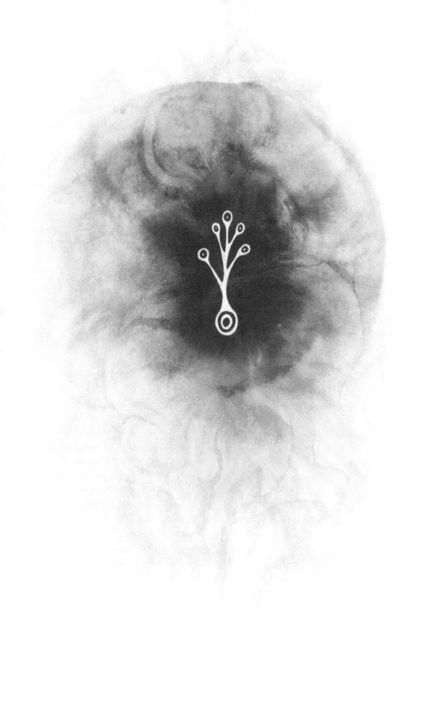

ANIMISM

Spirit lives everywhere

in all beings

in all things

not just human.

Hawk   and   Hemlock

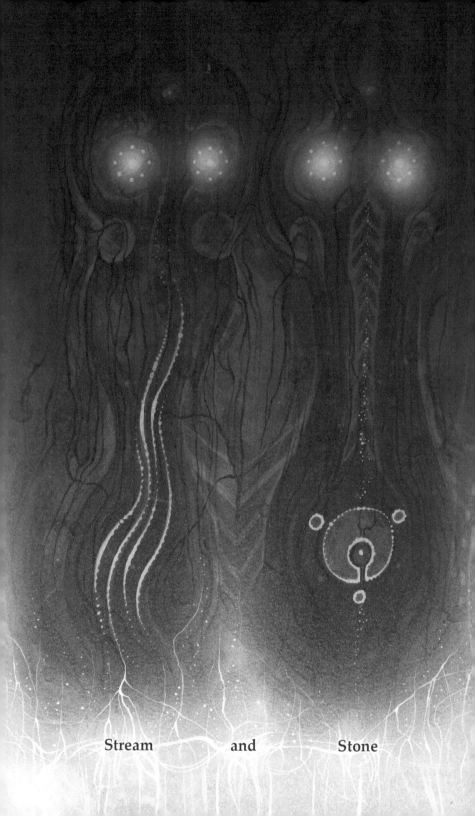

Stream   and   Stone

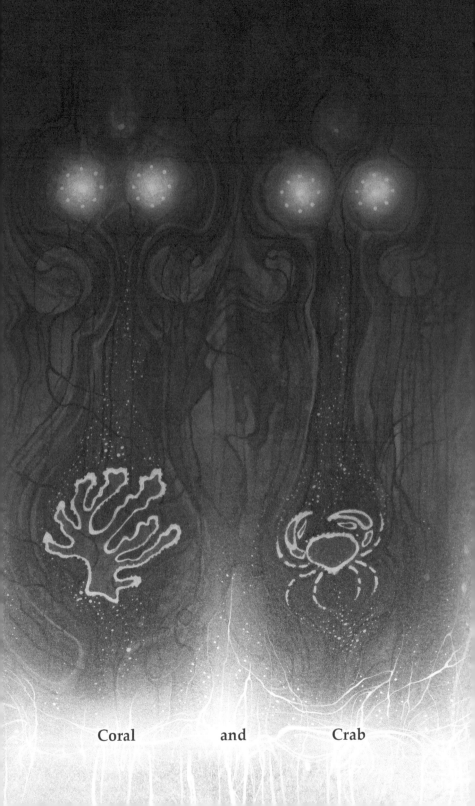

Coral   and   Crab

Snake and Soil

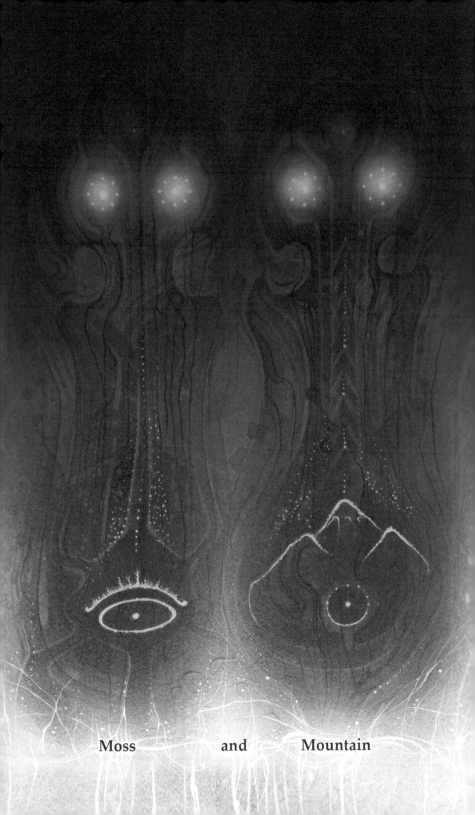

Moss   and   Mountain

Salmon   and   Seagrass

Fern and Firefly

Wind   and   Wildflower

All things live

All things have personhood

All are part of the Whole

Miracles

What is a miracle?
An amazing thing
    an extraordinary act
        an unexpected spark
            that leads to something good
                beyond all known powers?

A rare thing we think
so we would be blessed
to be in its presence even if
only once graced with good fortune

to feel the touch
of something divine to tell us
how special we are to be
present in that singular moment.

But what is a leaf
or a blade of grass?
Or the stalk of kelp rising tall
from the ocean floor?

What is the diatom floating free
in ocean currents?
They are all vessels for a miracle
neither rare nor sporadic.

The Fire of the Sun
that fuels transformation
of Air and Water into sugars
on which all life on Earth depends

and into oxygen that fuels the Mysteries.
So simple is this miracle to name,
this *photosynthesis*, this *making* by *light*.
So ordinary to eyes

that see only the green of the forest
or algae clinging to shoreline rocks.
But the green is merely
the outward flag that miracles

common as blades of grass
surround us, feed us,
support the Web
into which we are all bound.

Let air fill our lungs
and hearts beat with joy
and prayers spill unbidden
from our lips.

Spreading Life

Stand stone still in a field deep with flowers,
eyes closed against the blindness of light
yet ears open to the pulse of ecosystems in motion.
Ears open to rhythms fully hidden from sight.

Give praise to the small ones that form the foundation.
Give praise to the sounds that tell of their deeds.
Give praise to the insects who feed and move pollen.
Uniting with ova, the mothers of seeds.

Life as we know it depends on these small ones,
united together toward one common goal
of maintaining the system, the balance, the order,
supporting each function, creating the whole.

Creatures that perch higher up in the food chain
with talons and teeth that rend red and raw,
may seem so much larger than insects in meadows,
may claim they're invincible, and lord over all.

But the bees of the meadows, immune to such boasting,
know self-proclaimed lions come and go every year,
know the power that comes from mere pollination,
spreading life upon life and not fear upon fear.

What Lies Within

Take a seed,
hold it in your
hand, and with this
act you hold a universe.

A hard shell
gives it strength
and protects the soft
vulnerability of its core.

Means of movement
allow it to travel near or far,
riding wind or waves or animal
skin, alone or part of a larger whole.

An encoded library of skill
gathered from the past through
ancestors who spread, stretching
back down a story line to the dawn of life,

guiding it
on how to break its shell,
and let escape its growing
roots and leaves, to drink in

light and water,
to spur on growth,
code uniquely formed
by the lands and waters of home.

Skills that lead it through
its ages to the power to birth
more seeds and continue the story
so that it emerges to become an ancestor.

Look at this seed
in your hand and see in it all these things:

Strength
Vulnerability
Movement
Rootedness
Growth
Resilience
Knowledge
Connections intimate back into time
Connections intimate to the systems of life
And the urgency of continuance

Now look up
and change your gaze,
hold in your view a person:
a friend, an enemy, a parent, a child,

Or a complete stranger
who looks different than you,
or speaks with an unfamiliar tongue,
or who holds to different customs or beliefs.

Different words, different songs,
different ways of being in the Web.
Different prayers and dreams, different
knowings. Different gods, or no gods at all.

And see in them the seed.

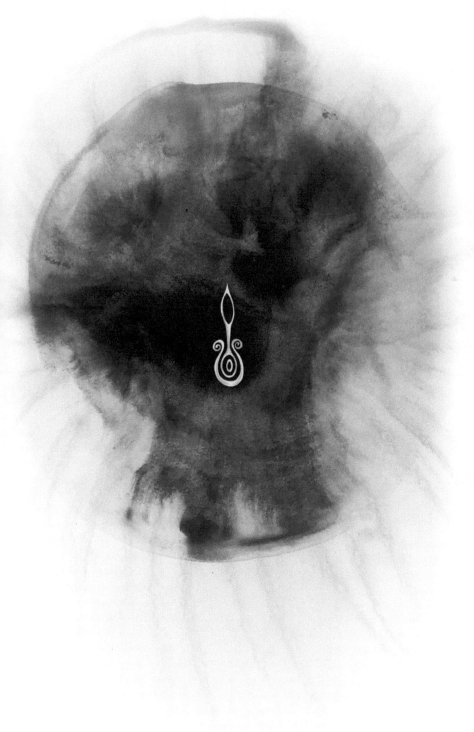

The Weaving

The Web's woven bones
include pain and blood.

Some you kill and eat.
Some would do the same to you

given chance, cause, or need.
Without the flow across beings,

the Web lies still, dead.
This too is a part of the Way of Gaia.

Millions of krill become humpback whales.
Kelp become urchins become otters then orcas.

Grubs become mice become spotted owls.
Roundworms feed fungal threads,

and flies become sundews.
The larvae of ichneumonid wasps

eat their way to the light
through still living hosts.

Just as grain and flesh become you.
Life and death woven together:

taking life gives life to the Web.
So it is, and so will it always be.

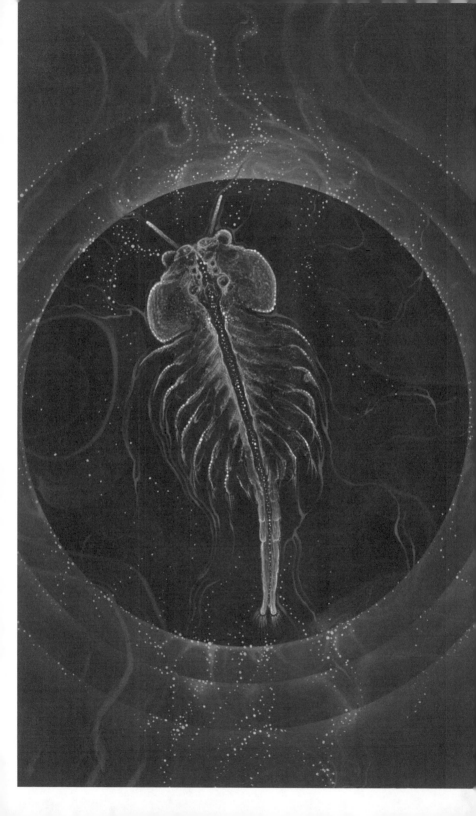

Closing the Gap

A Sperm Whale can hold its breath for an hour and a half,
diving almost two miles down, hunting food in forever
darkness and stunning prey with blasts of sound focused
by a sac of oil in its head.

A Ruby-throated Hummingbird can fly non-stop for
twenty hours across the Gulf from Alabama to the Yucatán
on less than a dime's weight of fat while its feathered
wings beat without rest a million times.

An African Lungfish can lie five years dormant buried in
mud, taking air through mucus spun to separate it from
time and the world until rains return to refill its home.

A Brine Shrimp can live in water nearly ten times saltier
than the ocean, killing conditions for all other life except
only a few forms of bacteria who live at the extreme edges
of existence on Earth.

∞

We exclaim at what they do, uniqueness
that defies our sense for the limits of life.

We hold them apart, allow difference
to create distance between Us and Other.

But look at yourself through their eyes and
sense their marvel at your difference from them.

A creative mind that imagines music and art,
time and space and the myriad paths of the Way.

Hands crafting tools to live underwater,
fly across oceans in hours not days,

induce life-saving comas lasting week upon week,
learning from others where the true limits lie.

We too are specialists, so let us move further
from distance and closer to marvel

at a world made grander by uniquity,
and let that bring All into union as One.

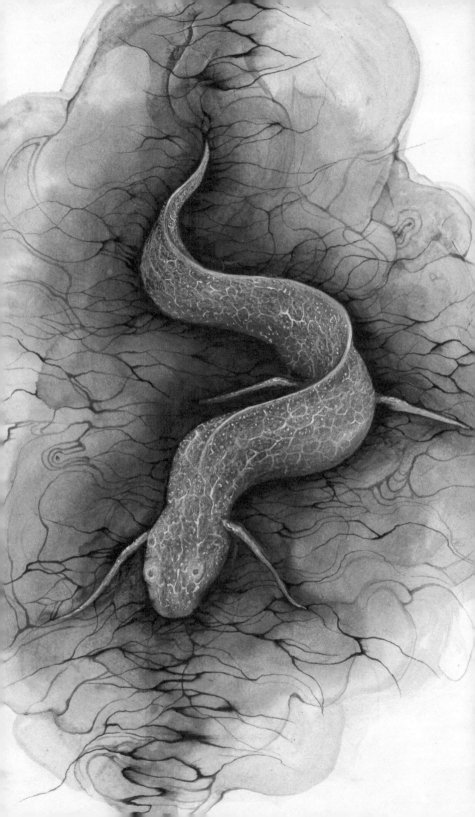

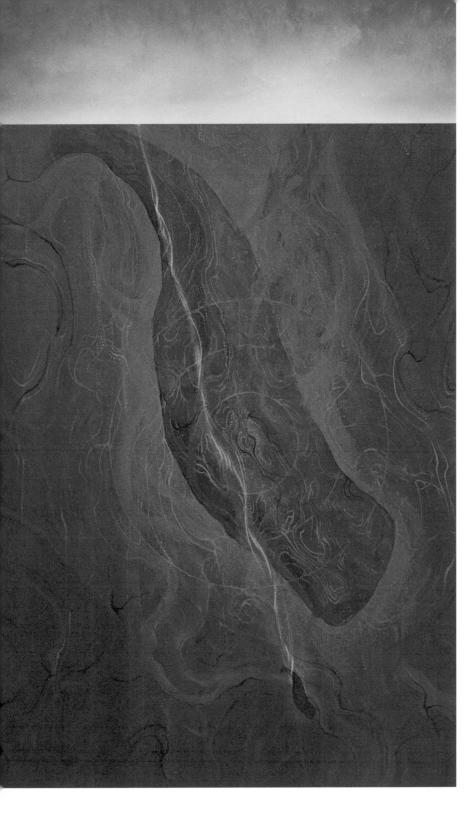

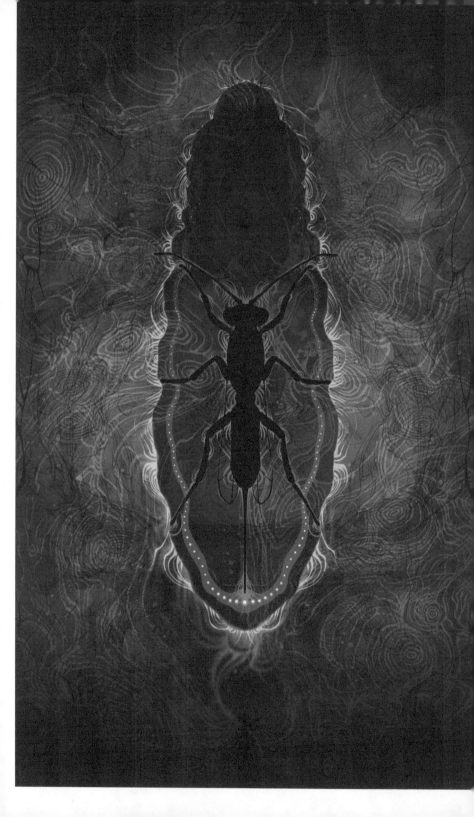

Dependence

Nature is not a metaphor.

The Way of Gaia is not a roadmap
always showing a One True Way
to live.

Life depends on life and in the Web
dependence paths
take many forms.

Some are shaped as unions so tightly
bound that neither lives
without the other.

Such is coral, symbiosis, alga giving oxygen
to polyp who in return gives
protection and food.

The acacia tree shelters ants who provide
protection against those who eat
or would compete.

One without the other means death for all.

Yet some involve unions on paths
of slow death to one as the other
eats or poisons from within.

The ichneumonid wasp lays its egg inside the body
of a larval butterfly and eats its way
out of the still living host.

Chaga fungus invades the body of a birch tree
and spreads throughout heartwood,
slowly feeding, decomposing.

One without the other means death.
One with the other
means death.

Nature is not a metaphor. It is that it is
and has come to include
many paths

not ours to judge, not ours to prevent,
not ours to follow if we are
to flourish.

Ours instead is to   Learn
                       Respect
                       Nurture
                       Protect

The hardest paths of all.

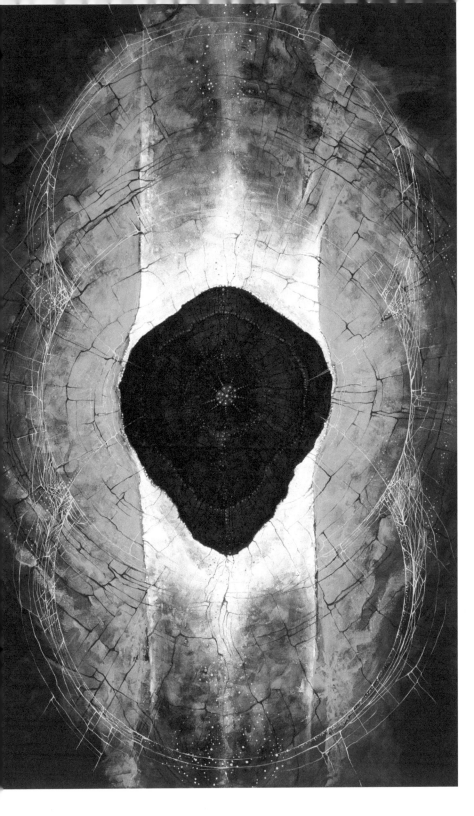

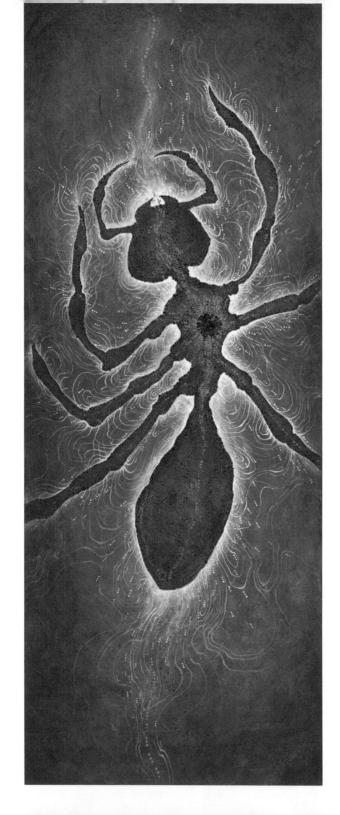

Collaboration

Call to mind your deepest desires,
the conditions of a life that lie close
within reach of enraptured perfection.

Who is with you in that precious place,
helping you thrive amid all the trials
and flourish long after you have arrived?

Do not be quick to answer lest your thoughts
fall short and miss the efforts
of all those there who keep you alive.

Who grows your food – *all* of your food –
supplies your water, your clothes, your light,
who by their labor helps you craft this life?

No matter how it is for you today or will be
for you tomorrow, you are there by the gifts
of others, just as they are by the gifts you bring.

What we have and all we desire
as a person, family, clan, or nation
can only be because we are with each other.

Without that, we have nothing.

Inner Connections

Consider your connections. Gaze inward
from the edge of your skin to see
that the essential you is a collective we.

Cells form tissues form organs form systems
in service with each other and in constant
communication through lines of transmission.

Be it chemicals coursing through blood like
letters written and sent, delivered and read to
maintain your wholeness in response or balance.

Kidneys craft vitamins needed to strengthen
bones and ignite the body's defenses
like ramparts against external invasion.

And in turn receive blood-borne commands to
balance your internal oceans, maintain pressure,
and sustain awareness.

So too the heart, flagged to race ahead or fall
behind by the signals received from molecules
released in the brain, skin, muscles, and lungs.

The brain, seat of perception and integration,
its parts bathed in a flood created or received,
driving urges and a constant wash of emotions.

Skin and gonads, lungs and guts, and all the senses,
react to the messages that shift the dials to grow,
breed, eat, digest, bank energy or set it afire.

Or be it electrical waves, a flow
along nerves, whip lines of ions rolling
like ripples out from a stone dropped in a silent pool.

Like dominoes falling forward to upend
a marbled cup, the impulse propels a message to
cross the gap where one nerve brushes ever so close

to the next and the next down the line, forking and
weaving through the body, demanding action or
reaction, forward propulsion or perfect silence.

Information from senses to brain to muscles
to senses. Information from every place to every
place in the constant call and response of living.

Remember this: You are a being of connections, made
whole by a web, fast or slow, reaching across synaptic
gaps and through membrane walls every moment.

Protect this web as if your life depends upon it.

Because it does.

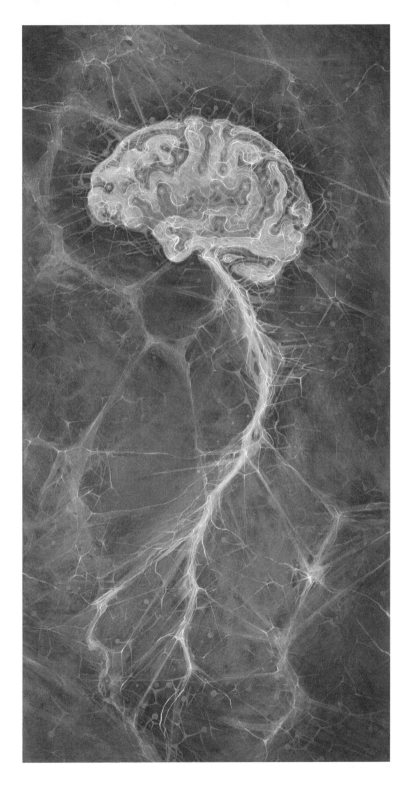

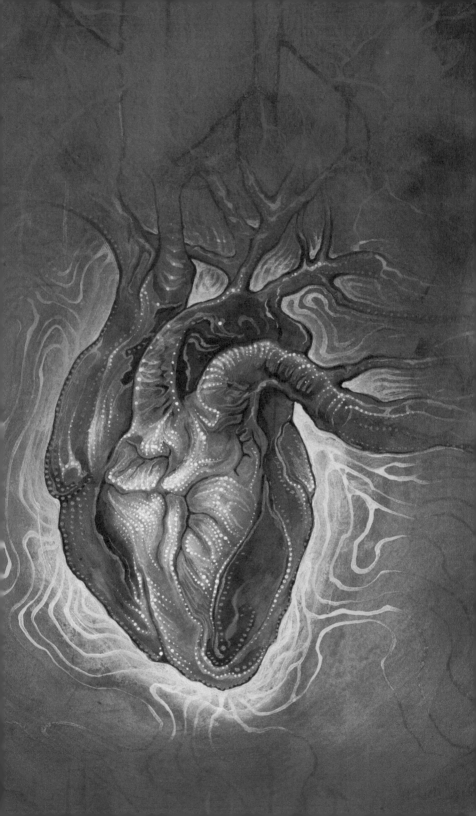

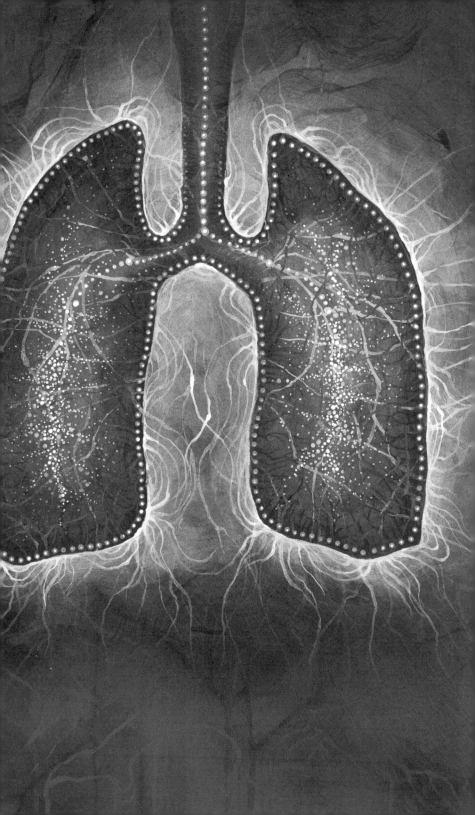

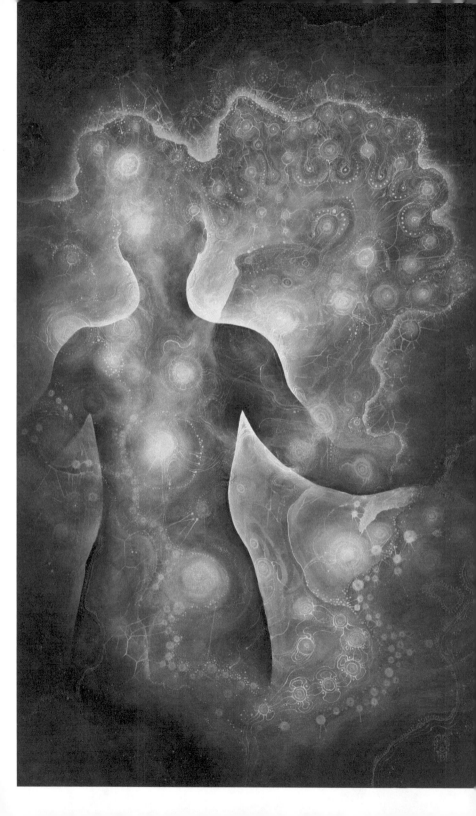

Outer Connections

Consider your connections.
Cast your mind's gaze out
from your skin to see the essential you

is a collective we.
The air of your in-breath
is the out-breath of plants

who in turn breathe in what you release.
The foods you eat are the bodies of beings
who were born and lived and died.

The wastes you make are broken down
by fungi and bacteria who feed the needs
for the emergence of new life.

The water you drink.
The heat you feel.
The firmness of ground.
The health of soil.
The resilience of your body.
The balance of your spirits.

All touched by the life around you.
All the life around you touched.
Carve at this life, allow it to slip away

even gently, and the touch weakens,
connections fade, and finally
so will you.

Positive Space

The edge of the forest, the edge of the sea,
the stream, the road, the meadow, the field,
the desert, the town, the edge of night,
of awareness, of sanity, of credibility.

We talk of edges as if they are endings,
as if what came before is now over
and what lies beyond is merely
the absence of what was named.

The edge becomes only a line between
what is and is not, where positive
space yields completely to negative
and crossing it is a step into the unnamed.

Yet the world is whole and functions as
a continuous flow, energy and matter
through and across the living web
that makes up the face of Gaia.

The forest and the meadow come together
and merge into each other's realms
just as the river glides to meet the bank
and the bank slips into the river's depths.

The sea rolls onto a shore of mud and sand
held fast by the roots of mangrove trees
that spread and thin away into the uplands
which themselves climb up into the mountains.

And at these meetings there occur more
than just a transition from one web
to another like the changing of a signal light
but rather there arises a profusion of life.

The birds and flowers of the forest
meet those of the meadow and create
a reach that is neither one nor the other
but an interweaving of both.

Fish of the sea swim into the tangled frame
of the mangrove roots to birth their young
even as monkeys and deer in the uplands
come down to scour the mangroves for food.

These meetings of ecological wholes
we call *ecotones*, once imagined
as places of tension, now known
as places of wealth.

When we seek to honor the life of Gaia
by needs we also include these ecotones
as valued parts of what it means to protect
and restore life on this sacred Earth.

But what if we took one more step along
the path that is the Way and brought
such awareness into all engagement
with each other and the world?

What if we re-envisioned all edges
as ecotones and valued them as those
in nature, places of meeting and melding,
enrichment and expansion?

What if we deliberately invited into cities
the more-than-just-human world to add its
vitality to that which we build, improving
the lives of all, from within and without?

What if we allowed our dreams to truly
fuel our waking world and actively
sought our dreaming states to pursue
insights and meaning in our conscious life?

What if the human community embraced
the qualities of all people across the span of
neurodiversity instead of assigning sides
across an imaginary edge of sanity?

What if, what if, what if? What if
we honored the existence of all ecotones?
Would we not then be more aware of the
deeper richness of our lives?

Would we not then name all existence
as positive space?

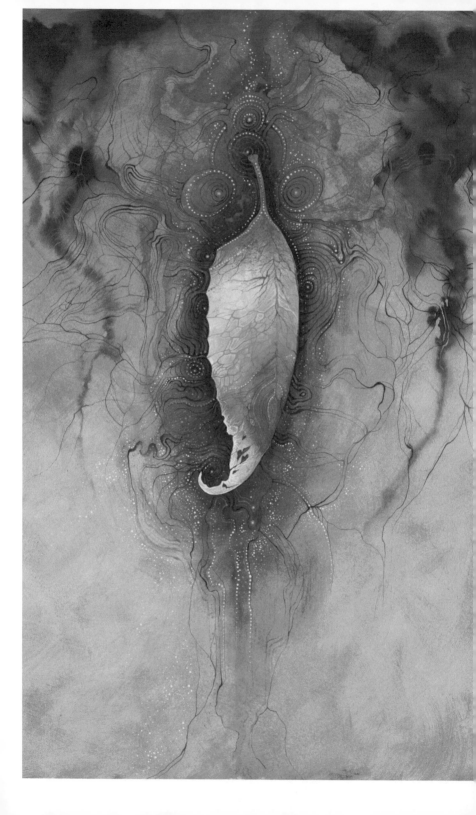

Decay

If I am to embrace life, I must also accept aging.
If I accept aging, I must acknowledge death.
If I acknowledge death, I must yield to decay.

In death, a body does not simply disappear.
Its lifestuff is broken apart and scattered,
transformed and transported to build anew.

All that lives is made of all that died.
All that dies feeds all that will live.
Both part of the indivisible Whole, eternal.

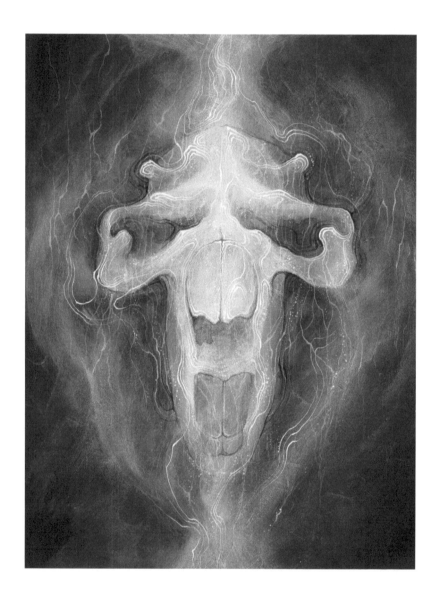

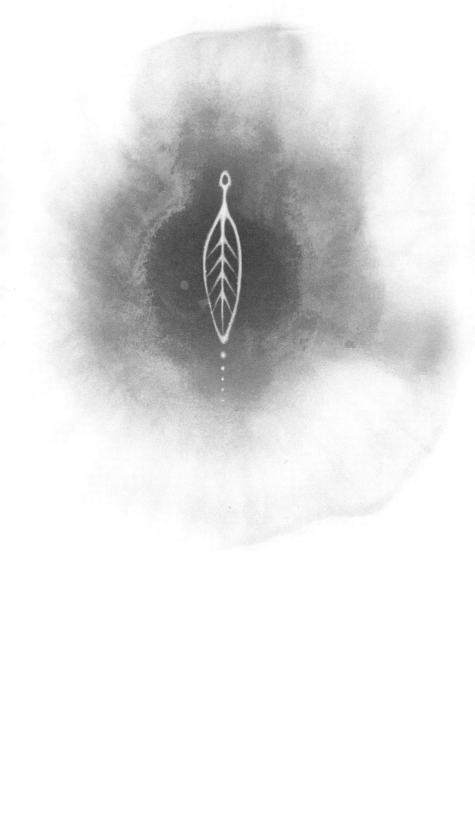

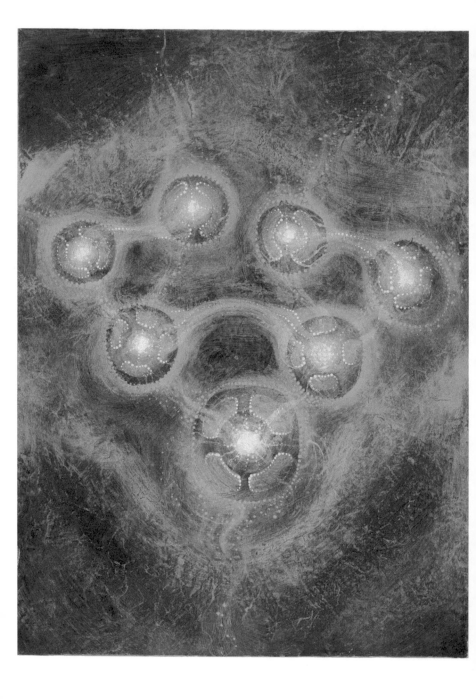

Who You Are

Consider who you are / Look deep
past your name, your job, your home,
past successes and failures, loves and hates,
beliefs and fears to look at the elemental

You.

Burrow all the way down to your animal self:
skin and muscles, bones and heart, brain and blood,
and trillions of cells that together make the organic
self, a priceless frame of your essential whole.

And consider again who you are / Knowing that
among all the billions of people alive today
and the hundred billion who have ever lived,
no one is or has ever been just like

You.

All because of your first spark / Egg and sperm,
the gifted union from your mother and father,
formed by a plan of mathematical precision and biological
drive laid down in the deep of time.

Doubling the strands that made each unique,
then dividing then halving so the egg and sperm
in union each gifted to the other only part
of who they were and in their union they made

You.

So consider again who you are / You are the child
of a knowing that stretches back a billion years.
The first emergence of a pattern linked to others
but unique in all the world and all of time.

You,

brought forth newly into the world.

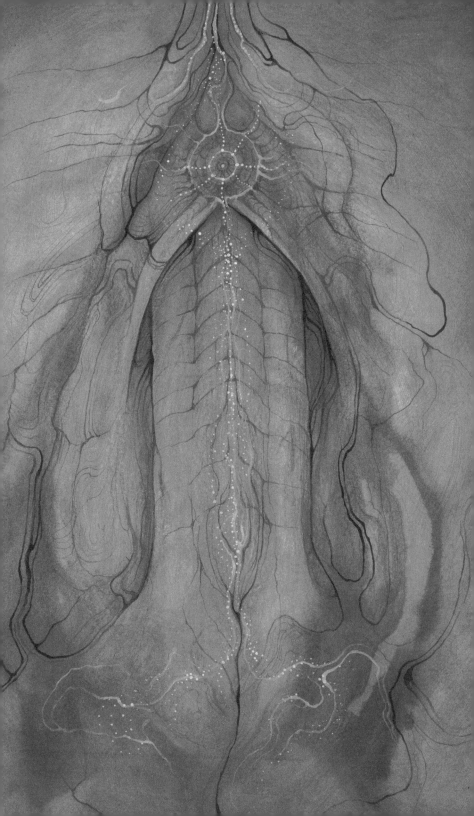

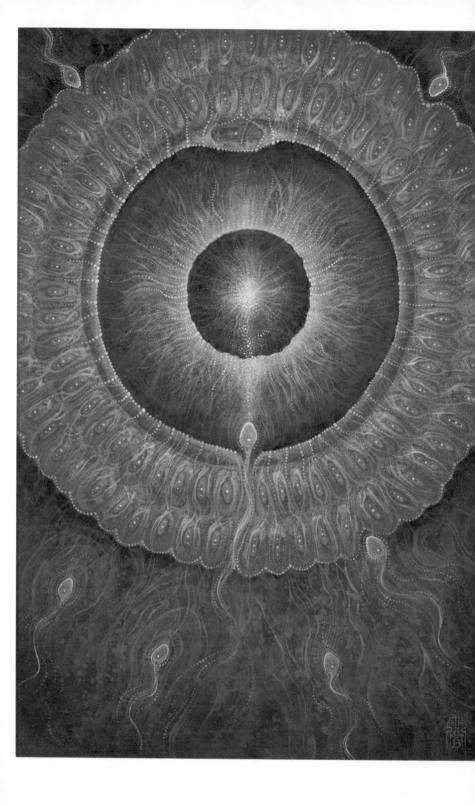

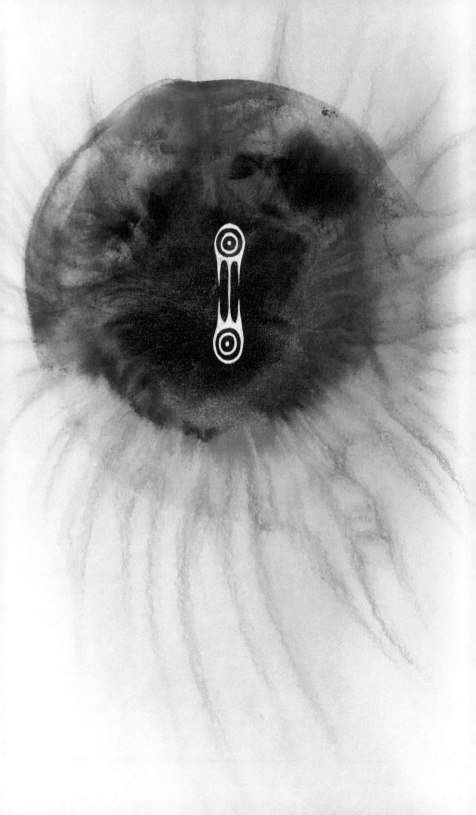

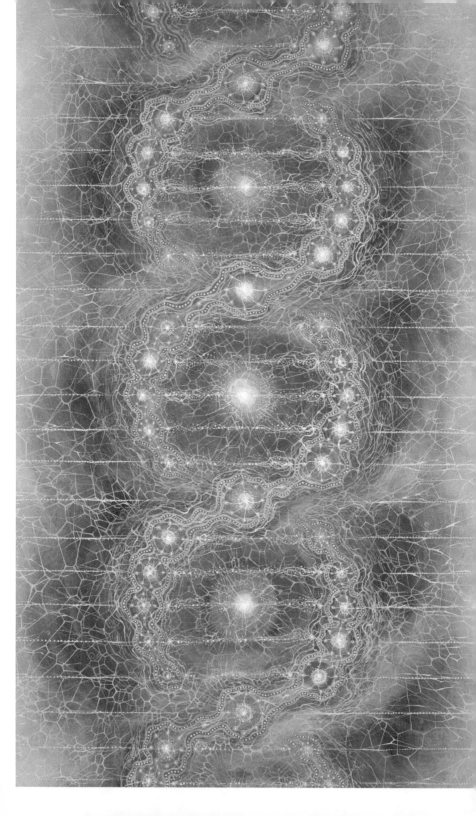

Woven in the Coils

Neither building block nor blueprint,
linked and twisted molecular strands
manifest the code that creates your form
and prepares you to be infused with spirit.

What you see when you look in a mirror
or gaze at your hands as they hold this page
is the miraculous result of the information
woven in the coils cradled in your cells.

That so simple of a structure, built from
a mere four themes of a molecular form,
can be the basis for the You that is created from
your parents' seed makes it no less miraculous.

The miracle comes from the order they
lie, like musical notes on a five-lined staff,
allowing infinite variation as sequences
translate into the machinery of life.

All the diversity that is now, has ever been, or will
ever be on the Tree is based on this simple truth:
pattern gives birth to information, which when
revealed sings the melodies and harmonies of Gaia.

Phoenix Rising

How often have you heard the phrase
"You're born, you live, you die" and thought
how clever it is to fold each soul
and the arc it travels into six simple words.

Hidden in this is an unspoken thought.
This cleverness speaks of only days,
time stretched from first breath to last
with life placed long or short neatly in between.

But life is not so simple, and sayings can ring
clear even if the reason is wrapped in mystery
played out too small and fast for naked eyes
to witness the miracles they would see.

We are born each moment across our span of
breaths and we die each moment alongside
each birth. The cells of our bodies fading
and flaming as from skin to soul we are reworked.

Each moment we are born anew, moving
forward from each death in each moment
before. Our cells know with atomic instinct
that we are always like the Phoenix.

Ever living.
Ever dying.
Ever rising.

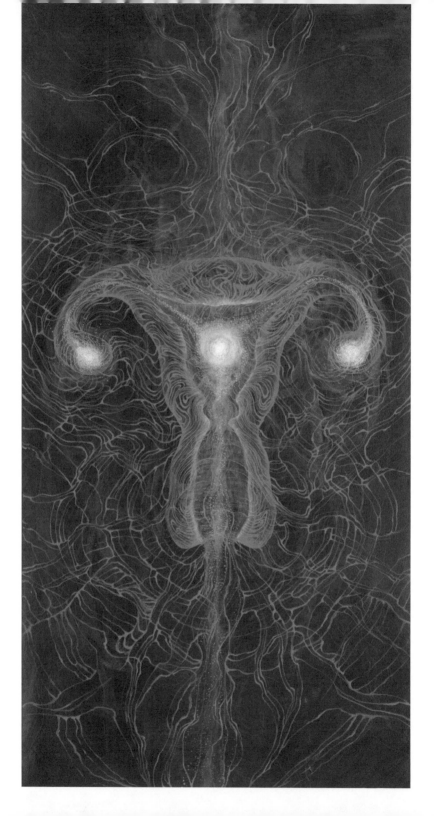

Into the Light

The pathway to becoming You
began in a saltwater sea
buffered against storms
and fed by a woman's blood.

Gentle your journey began
held in close embrace
by a rhythmic wash of heartbeat
and a symphony of voices.

The spark that would grow to
be your flame began just so
as a single cell complete
with a code just waiting to ignite.

One became two became four
then eight then more than need
be counted, stretching out as a
hollow ball to claim head and tail.

Cells migrated across and through
to turn you into a tube holding tubes,
your gut from mouth to anus
and the nerve cord that gave you sense.

Organs emerged and engaged,
instruments to maintain the internal
balance of your own saltwater sea
of blood and body.

Brain and nerves, heart and vessels,
kidney, lungs, liver, and gonads,
fingers and toes and hair and eyes
and every part integrated into You.

The Earth that became your body
and the Water that became your blood
had done what was needed in the womb,
now ready for your next step on the Path.

On signals too strong to ignore and
painful to bear, your time had come
to take in the Air that was your first
breath and heed your mother's call.

"Take this next step," she cried.
"Ignite the Fire that will be
your spirit through all your days
and come now into the light."

And so you did,
And so it was,
And so it is each day.
Always coming into the light.

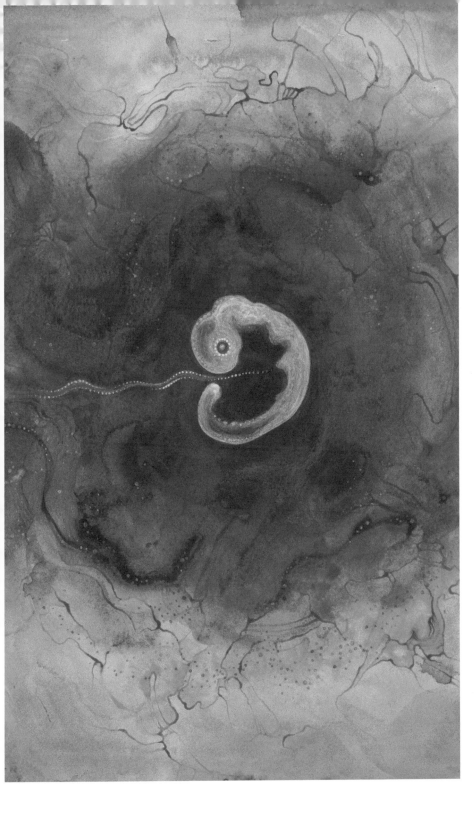

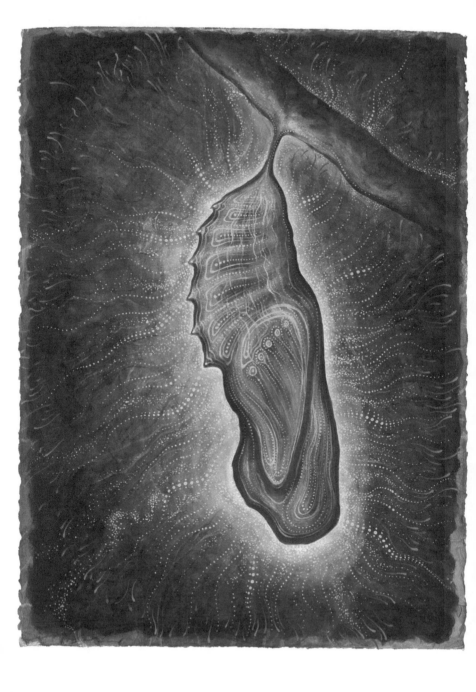

Change Comes to All Things

Today my prayer is this:

> As loss comes to all things,
>> May I gain wisdom in the places
>> made vacant by loss.

> As departure comes to all things,
>> May I find joy in each new arrival.

> As failure comes to all things,
>> May I see the successes that
>> the failures reveal.

> As sickness comes to all things,
>> May I work to strengthen health
>> in all beings.

> As darkness comes to all things,
>> May I train my senses to seek out
>> the light.

> As cold comes to all things,
>> May I embrace it as the state from which
>> warmth begins.

> As uncertainty comes to all things,
>> May I learn from all the possibilities
>> that uncertainty allows.

> As age comes to all things,
>> May I honor the journey from infant
>> to elder.

As death comes to all things,
    May I allow each passing to re-awaken
    my joy in each birth.

As decay comes to all things,
    May I use all the freed elements
    to build anew.

Today my prayer is this:

As change comes to all things,
    May I make each change
    a new beginning.

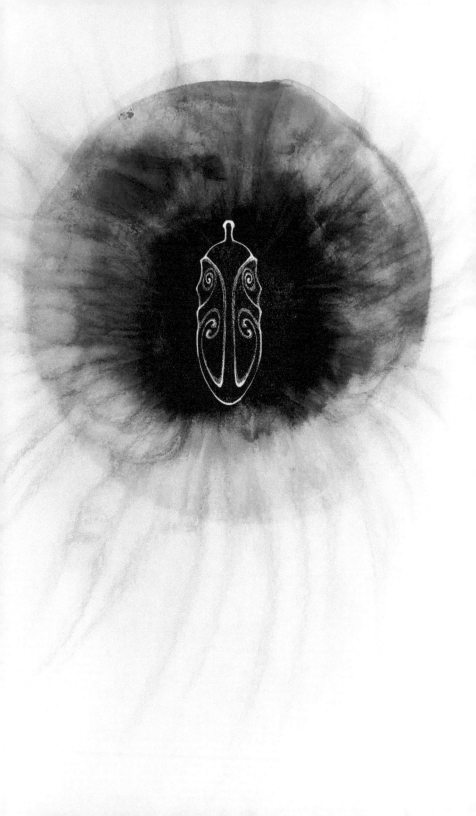

Senses

To know the world

her skin and blood
her body wild
unbound by borders
wet pulsing
pulled to depths
across spans
thick with spirit
embodied in
the personhood
of All Beings
open embrace
open to sky
open to passage
into your being

to know all this
your doorways
must open
and fully
attune

Touch

Reach out with every inch of your skin
into the Universe that reaches back to you.
Close your eyes.
Open your hands.
What do you feel?

Can you feel the warmth of those who reach back to hold
you?
Can you feel the unspoken truths under a soft caress?
Can you feel the brush of petals as you sweep across a
nearby flower?
Can you feel the smoothness of the stone lifted from the
river?
Can you feel the dampness of the earth that fills a garden?
Can you feel the pressure pulse as you tap out a rhythm?
Can you feel the rough edges built up from years of doing
what must be done?
Can you feel the strength of a circle with hands held tight?
Can you feel the gratitude in others when you lend yours
to help?
Can you feel all that can be accomplished when many
work together?

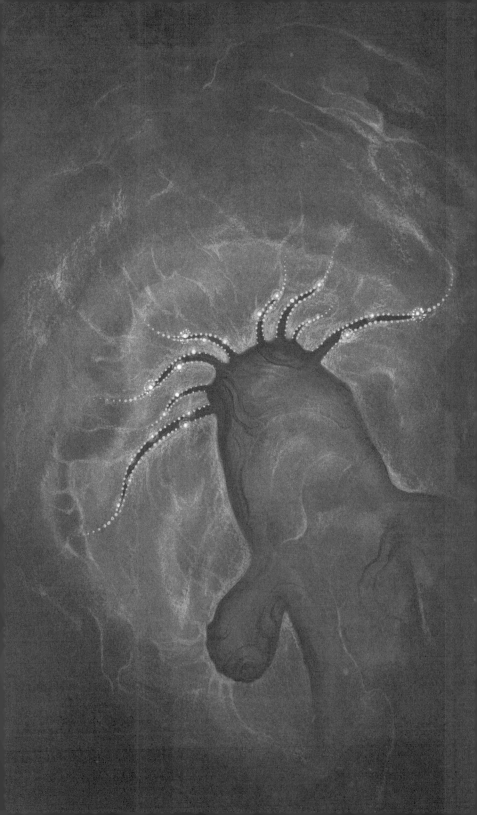

Taste

Reach out beyond your skin
into the Universe that reaches back to you.
Close your eyes.
Open your mouth.
What do you taste?

Can you taste the salt of your sweat as it rolls past your
 lips?
Can you taste the meal that you prepared with care and
 hunger?
Can you taste the air filled with the scent of one you love?
Can you taste the flavor of food taken fresh from the
 ground?
Can you taste the unique notes of the water that flows
 through your home's watershed?
Can you taste the difference between that which is clean
 and that which is not?
Can you taste the joy on the skin of loved ones you kiss?
Can you taste your blood's iron as you lick your wounds
 and prepare for more?
Can you taste the bile as it rises in your throat when you
 see injustice?
Can you taste the winds of change as they rush toward you
 unbidden and demand that you heed?

Scent

Reach out beyond your skin
into the Universe that reaches back to you.
Still your heart.
Breathe in deep.
What do you smell?

Can you smell the musk of the papers you hold?
Can you smell the sweat that seeps from your pores?
Can you smell the essence of flowers luring in bees?
Can you smell the bees, laden with pollen?
Can you smell the coming of rain and the coming of
    spring?
Can you smell the life that infuses the damp earth at your
    feet?
Can you smell the location of food and whether it is safe to
    eat?
Can you smell the difference between feast and famine?
Can you smell the fear in all those for whom hunger is
    constant?
Can you smell their relief when your hand reaches out to
    help?

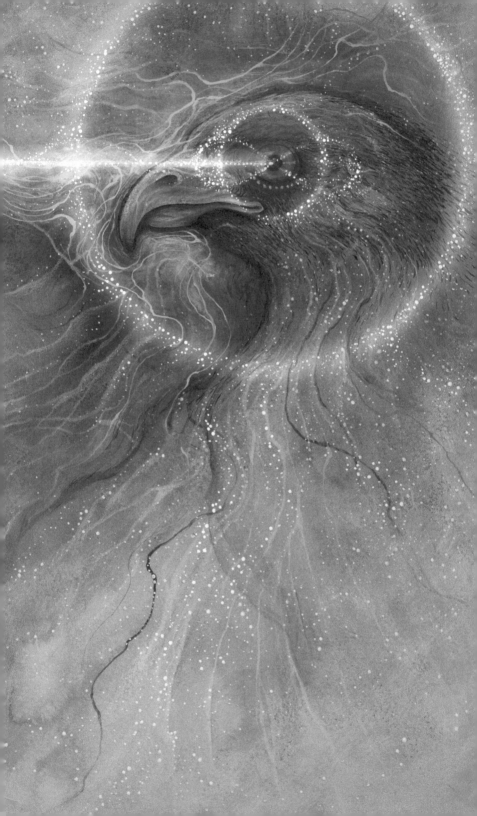

Sight

Reach out beyond your skin
into the Universe that reaches back to you.
Still your mind.
Open your eyes.
What do you see?

Can you see the sky as a glow spreads with the rising sun?
Can you see the life of the world apart from humanity's
face?
Can you see the failings in those you love and still love
with all your heart?
Can you see the passion and strength that beam out from
each person you meet?
Can you see the seasons change across the broad arc of
time?
Can you see the remains of the choices you've made, and
from them learn what needs to be learned?
Can you see what in truth lies before you, separate from
bias and fear?
Can you see what lies beyond your next step or choice?
Can you see how much stronger we are if we all see each
other?
Can you see how much our lives depend on us all seeing
clearly?

Sound

Reach out beyond your skin
into the Universe that reaches back to you.
Close your eyes.
Hold your breath.
What do you hear?

Can you hear the atoms beating inside your ears?
Can you hear your pulse, a signal of the life that flows
    inside you?
Can you hear the birds singing out to claim their places in
    the world?
Can you hear the air moving from the Sun's urging?
Can you hear the ground moving, crust sliding, and
    magma rolling?
Can you hear the Earth's steady vibrations?
Can you hear the passage of time?
Can you hear the love that surrounds you, calling your
    name soft but clear?
Can you hear the cries of others, asking for aid and
    understanding?
Can you hear your own voice, inside your heart, deciding
    what you will do next to give voice to those without?

Magnetism

Reach out beyond your skin
into the Universe that reaches back to you.
Close your eyes.
Hold your breath.
Which way is North?

Can you feel the pull of the magnetite crystals housed in
    your brain?
Can you feel the lines of attraction that flow 'round the
    Earth?
Can you feel the rising of the Sun and the coming of day?
Can you feel the burning of the auroras in the night sky?
Can you feel how birds will move on high when the
    seasons change?
Can you feel the pull that guides sea turtles on their ocean
    journeys?
Can you feel where you are in relation to home?
Can you feel the directions from which storms will
    descend?
Can you feel where to go with the coming of change?
Can you feel how to lead your people to safety?

Patterns

Take a walk in the outside and feel yourself in the presence of the Other. The more-than-just-human world. Let your eyes pass with soft gaze over the scene before you and come to rest in one place that reveals something that is of nature. As your mind settles, two thoughts will quickly rise about what you see, perhaps without you even being aware, thoughts that write the language of its being as it speaks to you:

How does it appear? / Its nouns and adjectives
How does it behave? / Its verbs

Everything you see in the world – biological or physical – exists within this language of sentences parsed into the clauses of form and action.

Now with intention invite a third thought to emerge. How do these clauses interact to manifest pattern? Intimately linked through time, measured as fast as the resonant transition of an atom or as slow as eons of evolutionary change, they create dynamic meaning. Linked by the ceaseless forces that drive the movement of energy and matter, or the drive to survive and reproduce despite the odds against either. How does pattern come into being to create the essential self of all that is?

Come into communion with all those around you – the plants, animals, stones, and waters. Come into awareness of their personhood and see their essential being, the languages they speak by their forms and actions. Their whats and whys. Their patterns.

Spirals :
Coiling outward of a large volume
released from constraint in a smaller space,
as the unfurling of a frond, the axial wrap
of a shell, or the arms of a galaxy trailing
after the spinning core.

Waves :
Ripples flowing outward from an energetic locus, as a
pebble cast in a pond, a spoken word, or a candle flame.

Spheres :
A deceptively simple shape with each point on its surface
the same distance from its center allowing the least
surface area for a volume, promoting balance and
stability over time, as in a bubble, rain drop, egg yolk,
fruit, and even the Earth itself.

Lines : The streamline flow of energy acting upon matter,
moving water in a river, sap in the vessels of a tree
trunk, lava down a mountain slope,
and glacier ice through a valley.

Branches : Networks of connection allowing for the maximum spread of pathways with the least amount of material, as in blood vessels, lung passages, tree canopies and roots, and riverine flows.

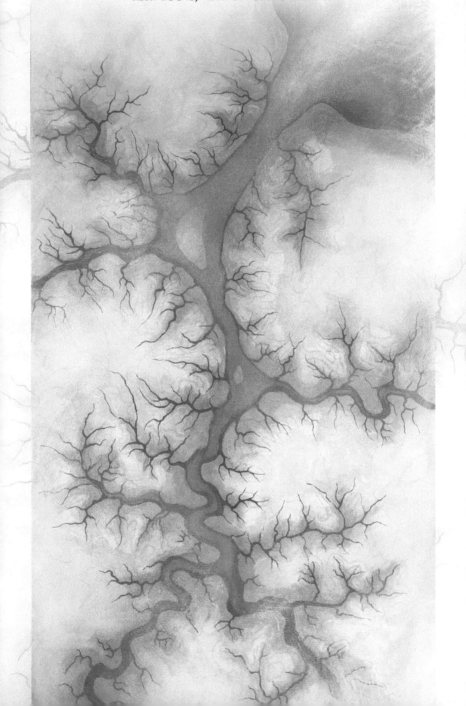

Webs : Patterns of connection among points or objects, as with the real connections of threads in a spider web and the flow of energy among species in a food web.

Lobes : Increasing useful edge with the increasing size that
comes with growth, capturing the benefits of both
in brains, lungs, leaves, and the fruiting bodies of fungi.

Scales : Flexible sheets of protection
like the bracts of a pine cone, the skin of a fish,
the legs of a bird, the armor of a Pangolin,
or the iridescent covering of a butterfly's wings.

Scatter : Dispersion by explosion to increase spread and
ward off attack, like seeds from a Touch-me-not even
only gently brushed and from the Sandbox Tree
when its fruit fully ripens, or the release
of egg and sperm from an urchin.

Clouds : Slow and undirected diffusion of one material into another, as water vapor condensing into droplets in the sky and silt breaking away from the banks of a river.

Overbeck Jets :
Whirlpools and eddies spiraling into themselves
as fluids meet resistance flowing past fixed objects,

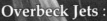

as water along a stream bank, wind through
a forest, smoke rising through a chimney,
mud-filled rivers meeting the ocean, and warm air
rising into denser layers of the atmosphere.

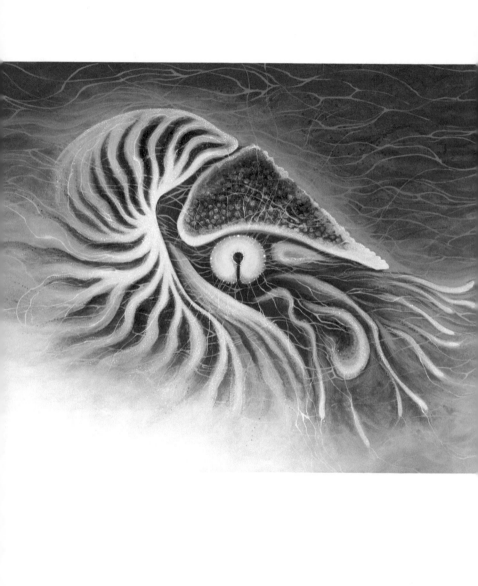

Forever Gone

Sing praise for the nautilus:

Deep tropical swimmer,
fringe feeder on reefs,
descendant of lines
that stretch back unbroken,
500 million
sun-centered journeys,
back from the dawn
of all complex life.

Sing praise for the nautilus:

Tentacled arms
reach out from its spiral,
crabs grasped and pulled
to a parroted beak,
movement precise
like a jetted balloon,
rising and dropping
over thousands of feet

Sing praise for the nautilus:

Strong and resilient,
survivor of chaos
both great and wild
that extinguished so many,
survivor of fire,
volcanoes, and star storms
of acid and ash,
spreading darkness and death.

Sing praise for the nautilus:

> As it slides to extinction,
> killed for the luster
> of its interior shell,
> sectioned and carved
> into bangles and pearls,
> faster than young
> can replace all those taken,
> dying for art,
> dying for beauty,
> dying for praise
> more in death than in life.

Sing praise as we watch

> them all pass on to extinction,
> erased from the Tree,
> only shells left behind
> as mementos and memories
> of their lives in the ocean,
> dead beauty replacing
> their fullness of life.

Sing praise for them all:

> White ferula mushroom, the mountain gorilla
> Underground orchid, the sturgeon, the rhino
> The leopard, the hawksbill, saola, vaquita
> The pangolin, tiger, Lyndenburg cycad
> African elephant, elegance coral
> Toyama's ground gecko
> Cabezón de añavingo
> Ploughshares tortoise
> Escobilla de masca
> *Euastacus dalagarbe*
> Cowen's mantilla
> Oceanic whitetip
> Diademed safika
> *Tilapia bythobates*
> Nassau grouper
> Philippine croc
> Myaka myaka
> Manara
> 'Akoko
> Nehe
> Alani

Sing praise for them all

> in their thousands of thousands,
> fading like day,
> cut from the Tree,
> forever passing away.

Human Footprint

Our footprints are pressed deep
and deeper still so that soon
we may not walk at all.

Nor oak tree grow.
Nor orca hunt.
Nor kelp forest sway.
Nor minnow dart.

Nor owl glide silent.
Nor vine climb.
Nor hibiscus bloom.
Nor coral build.

Nor river flow.
Nor fern unfurl.
Nor microbes feed
the soil as food.

Nor frogs fill the night,
nor warblers the day.
Nor bees spread pollen.
Nor sea otter play.

Nor plankton fix from the bottom up.
Nor wolf bare teeth and push top on down.
Nor fungus move cycles that drive all life.

With conscious mind, walk lightly, tiptoe gently.
Then perhaps we can all walk together.

Butterfly Effect

So, there's this poem by Taylor Mali
and I want to tell you about how
it changed my life.

The story can be told in two ways.
There's the long version and the short version.
And the long version goes something like this:

So, there's this poem by Taylor Mali called
The Problem. It's not one of his funny sarcastic
"Yeah, I've *so* been there" poems

about teachers making and writer's writhing
and speakers speaking, you know, like badly?
The Problem is one of those B-side poems

that never made it onto YouTube
or into the spotlight 'cause it lacks
the kind of high-minded flare

that lets it kill when the stage is hot,
the best has been brought,
and each voice burns as if on fire.

The Problem is a simple poem about Mali trying
to get on a train in New York City. And he can't
'cause the guy in front of him won't move.

But Mali sees that the guy in front of him
is not *the* problem. He's *my* problem,
Mali says, but he's not *the* problem.

The problem is the guy further up the line
who won't step aside to let anyone pass and
becomes the wellspring of cascading problems

flowing back along the line turning
the platform, train, and people into a complex
system whose behavior is totally screwed

by that one guy, *the* problem,
who makes everyone else
someone else's problem.

It's a good poem and you should read it sometime.
But that's not why I'm telling you
this story or how it changed my life.

I'm a teacher, you see, and not
in some vague metaphysical sense.
I have real students who pay real money

for me to teach them something
they could not learn on their own even if
they bothered to read the textbook.

I get paid to help them see
what's *really* in front of them.

So the other day I was teaching this class
about the environment and the fate of the world
and how their generation must do better than mine.

But everything is connected to everything else and
seeing the right lever, solution, or incantation
means you have to see what's really going on.

154

Consider this: The solution to pollution in
Lake Baikal may in fact *not* be another wastewater
treatment plant but instead may be

an easing of ethnic conflict in Nigeria because
of the chain of effects that ripple out from Africa
like oil through pipelines, banks, and backroom deals.

It's about the connections between the seafood
sold by Wal-Mart and deaths in Thailand when
tsunami waves crush mangrove-stripped villages.

It's about the connections between
clear-cutting in Ecuador and drought in India.
Between gold mining, nutrition, and health.

Between energy, babies, and clean water.
Between cars, charcoal, and asthma.
Between the beat of a butterfly's wings and *everything*.

Each of our lives and tribes are enmeshed in a web
so complex in time and space that our minds
can only contain it all by simply calling it

Mother Earth and emoting metaphorically about her
as if she were a single thing rather than the
dynamic chaotic ball of non-linear loops she really is.

And that is *so* hard to teach! I show PowerPoint
slides replete with six-color graphs on AIDS
in Uganda and salt in fields of Australian wheat.

Rates of extinction and the rise in everything
from CO_2 concentrations to suicide rates to cancers
in children who live in the wrong part of town.

And it's like I am speaking in tongues,
a language for my students that is
completely unknown and completely unknowable.

And it breaks my heart.

So anyway, one day, before the start of class
I decide, what the hell, I'll read a poem.
I bring poems to poetry circles,

why not to my science class, right?
I read *The Problem*. It's a good poem.
I like it. They like it. We move on.

Days later, on a field trip to a local park
I'm walking behind two of my students
eavesdropping in that silent way that teachers do

to learn what they are really thinking
and not just what they want you to think they're
thinking. And one says to the other,

"I don't get the reading. First, it's about Antarctica
melting, then its rivers flooding in Asia, polar bears
dying, and Third World debt. I don't see what the
point is supposed to be."

And the other one says, "Dude, it's like in that poem.
Don't just look at *a* problem. Look for *the* problem.
The guy in the subway who won't step aside."

Silence ensues, and finally the first one says, "Oh,
I get it. Earth is the subway. It's a system and
you have to find *the* problem to make a change."

And finally, after all these years, after all
the six-colored graphs and ten-column tables,
the spreadsheets, worksheets, peer-reviewed papers,

problem sets, mock debates, clickers, and classrooms
flipped upside down and inside out, because of
poetry, I have finally taught somebody something.

So that's how a poem changed my life.

A poem is more than an invitation to enjoy
a brief bit of syncopated word play.
A poem is a window, a doorway, a Rubik's cube

right on the edge of being solved and showing
a whole new way to see the world. And now
I will always start my classes with a poem.

Because that's how a poem changed *their* lives.
They're now looking, really looking
to find *the* problems.

And maybe, just maybe a poem will change
your life. Because those two students, or
ones just like them, may one day save the world.

So that's the long version of the story.
The short version goes something like this:
"You are a butterfly. Be mindful of how you beat your
wings."

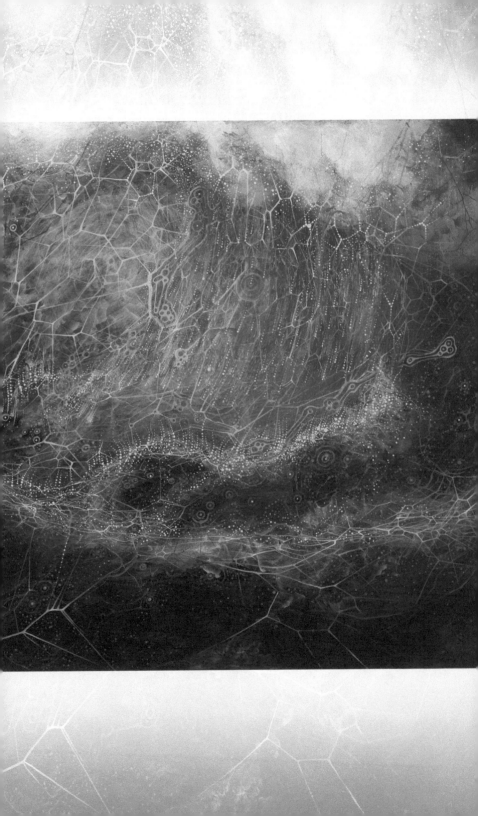

The Strength of Gaia

As Gaia provides energy through her winds and waters and by permitting the passage of sunlight through her air, may we use energy within her capacity to sustain us.

As Gaia provides forests and plankton that can absorb carbon dioxide, may we release carbon dioxide through our actions only within her capacity to maintain balance.

As the plants of Gaia's land and seas produce oxygen that sustains all life, may we live in peace with them and allow them to flourish in their own ways across her face, from her summits to her depths.

As Gaia provides fungi and wetlands that can destroy poisons on land and in waters, may we protect them from harm and release poisons only as much and in kind as is her capacity to cleanse.

As Gaia provides soils and rains that allow edible plants to flourish, may we grow our food only within her capacity to sustain us.

As Gaia holds vast ocean basins home to the multitudes of those who swim, may we harvest from these waters only within her ability to replace those who are taken.

As food webs across Gaia's face are tuned through the actions of predators who balance the flow of numbers among all others, may we respect their existence so that balance is maintained.

As Gaia renews the land through floods and weathering, may we alter the land only within her capacity to build anew.

As Gaia provides vast stores of freshwater in the underground, may we withdraw from them for our own uses only as fast as she can replenish them, and may we treat the lands above in ways that do not limit her ability to do so.

As Gaia has the strength to allow all peoples to flourish now and forever, may we choose to live always within the limits of her strength.

Anthropocene

You can see it in the eyes of the young mother who has learned that the cancer has spread throughout her body and that she will never live to see her child start their first day at school, or fall in love, or become a parent.

You can read it in the numbers on the face of the Geiger counter pegged at the highest value it can display, even more than 35 years after the blast and 20,000 years before it will be safe to enter again.

You can taste it in the air as the sea washes further onto the island each year, each surge drowning more villages, more fields, telling those who live there that their home is forever gone.

You can sense it in the stony stillness of Martha, the last Passenger Pigeon to live, now stuffed and perched for museum display, trying to will those who see her that this is what carnage without care for the future can bring.

You can smell it on the fur and breath of the Timber Wolf released with purpose back into the Wild to bring balance to a landscape whose web became twisted and scarred after wolves had been hunted to oblivion out of fear and greed a century before.

You can hear it in the footsteps of the people as they march for days across winding rural roads, demanding change against the rising crisis of the warming planet.

You can feel it in the will of the child who says they will only choose what to eat, how to stay warm, and where to live so that they can help restore balance to the Earth.

The Way of Gaia

All this and more.
In the reach of time and space
across the fullness of Gaia's body,
no teaching yields instruction
for every step along your Path.

Each moment offers
a choice of how to travel,
and the choice is always yours.
The Way of Gaia is not a code
on what choice to make
but in how to make it.

Self   Respect
Family   Love
Tribe   Peace
Species   Honor
Life   Aware
Pattern   Thanks
Time   Flow
Spirit   Grace
Change   Protect
Union   Connect
Balance   Energy

Interwoven lines linking
circles within circles of kinship
and the cultivated voice of your soul.
Gaia's gift is not a waymark on a map
but a light to help you find your way.

May her light guide you
with every step.

Gratitudes

This book—in both what it presents and how it presents it—is an encapsulation of our lifetimes of learnings, practice, and experience. It is therefore no exaggeration to say that we are grateful to everyone with whom we have ever come into contact, whether it be in person, through their writings, or by their examples. However, some people and groups deserve special acknowledgement......

♥ EarthSpirit Community, for being the nucleus to start our many years of creative collaboration and a place to express freely our reverence for the spirit of the Earth with a community of like-minded souls.

♥ Lis McLoughlin, for editing and publishing, patience and prodding.

♥ erin feldman, for her critical but loving eye in review.

From Martin, especially ...
♥ George Leighton Bridge, for fostering a love of nature and art; U Barbara Bridge, for nurturing my path; and Carl Bridge, for walking together, and challenging and supporting one another in our creative pursuits.

♥ Rosalie, Leah, and Issa, for their support and encouragement during the major push to complete this project.

♥ The Permaculture Elders and Mentors, especially Delvin Solkinson, for giving me the framework to meet my reverence for the Web of Life with practical action.

♥ Jim Gipe, for capturing my work so artfully that it can be shared with you now.

♥ The artists I have studied under and worked next to, for their help in the refinement of my craft.

♥ My Patreon supporters, for helping me prioritize this work.

And from Steve …
♥ Joss Price, for always being with me on this journey, no matter how long or where it led.

♥ Anne Haven McDonell, for poetic guidance.

♥ My distributed network of family and friends, for their contributions to the entries on the Elements.

♥ The community of spoken word poets of Soul Expressions at SpiritFire Festival, for being awesome logophiles.

♥ Over 2,000 students of natural history, environmental science, and conservation biology, for joining me on a journey of discovery.

♥ Michael Soulé, Dave Foreman, and Reed Noss, for making a love of the Wild an external howl and not merely a private reflection.

♥ Aldo Leopold, for writing *The Land Ethic.*

—*Steve Trombulak & Martin Bridge*

Our Paths

Martin Bridge, born into a lineage of artists, educators, and nature lovers, began his days in the woodlands and wetlands along the edge of the Charles River. From an early age, art became his primary vehicle to explore and contemplate the world around and within him, and it continues to hold that place for him today.

Having stumbled into the realm of theater when asked to create paintings and sculptures for a play, he instantly became enthralled with various visual artforms and how they could be entwined into a living experience.

Martin had a series of revelatory experiences while traveling in Japan and the Rocky Mountains in 1991 that began for him a spiritual journey. Inexplicable experiences at Koyasan and an encounter with a brown bear led him to a search for greater understanding.

While serving as Scenic Designer for a production of "Dancing at Lughnassa," he began to explore European Paganism. This eventually led him to the EarthSpirit Community, where he first encountered Steve behind a drum by firelight, now 25 years ago.

To be closer to his tribe of spirit, he moved to the foothills of the Berkshires of Western Massachusetts. There he began to dive deeply into Permaculture Design and Mycology. Teaching at a school that sought to break traditional academic boundaries, he began to seek greater connections between art and science. The search to bridge the spaces between the aesthetic and rational is a major pursuit in his work today.

Steve Trombulak grew up near the tidepools of coastal California, opening the door to his path as a curious observer of the natural world. Yet it was time spent among the high peaks of the Range of Light that led him to a feeling of kinship with—and responsibility toward—the Wild. Curiosity about the natural world led him to a B.A. in Biology (UCLA), a Ph.D. in Zoology (U. Washington), and postdoctoral research in Biological Sciences (Stanford U.). In those combined years, he studied pine trees, rodents, hummingbirds, and beetles in deserts, tropical forests, and mountain tops.

Moving to the other side of North America, he joined the faculty of Middlebury College, teaching biology and environmental studies for 34 years. There, he gravitated into the field of conservation biology, working with many like-minded colleagues on wildlands conservation and protection in North America and supervising research projects on several different species, ranging from sea lamprey to wolves. He is an author or editor of five previous books, all related to natural history and conservation. He retired as Professor Emeritus from Middlebury College in 2019.

Despite a childhood connection with a mainstream Western religion, his engagement with ecological science and conservation advocacy led him to a more earth-centered spiritual practice, one best described simply as *animism*: the belief that humans are not the only beings with spirit. This brought him into community with others who share similar beliefs, where he met Martin, who said, "Why don't we develop a book together—my art, your words—about the spirit of Gaia?" To which he said, "Great idea. Let's do it!"

Art Index

Original works for sale and fine art prints of many of the artworks are available through:
https://www.thebridgebrothers.com

If you would like to support Martin's art visit:
https://www.patreon.com/martinclarkbridge

Printed in the USA
CPSIA information can be obtained
at www.ICGtesting.com
LVHW061642151123
763888LV00026B/86/J